CROCHET FOR BEGINNERS

The Ultimate Step-by-Step guide on How to learn crochet in an easy way

(With Pictures – 2nd Edition)

MARY STITCH

sources. Please consult a licensed professional before attempting any technique outlined in this book.

By reading this document, the reader agrees that under no circumstances is the author responsible for any losses, direct or indirect, which are incurred as a result of the use of the information contained within this document, including, but not limited to, errors, omissions, or inaccuracies.

Table of Content

Introduction

Crochet is one of the most beautiful pastimes of all time.

The image associated with this art is often that of the grandmother who spends her days carrying out her work in front of the window or a fireplace. Today it is very popular, and there are many people who, for the first time, approach this fantastic world, thanks to their mothers and grandmothers.

With the changes in society that have taken place over the years, the way of seeing and making crochet has also changed. Also, thanks to the advent of technology and, above all, to that of social media, one of the hottest things is certainly to post your works and show them to the whole world.

In this book, we will take a path that starts from the history of crochet and then moves on to theory (materials and techniques of crochet among the rest that will be covered), and finally to practice as only by applying what you will learn you will be able to appreciate up to fund this art.

Chapter 1: The History of Crochet

Theories

Annie Potter—a world traveler, and crochet expert—said that crocheting started in the 16th century. Back then, it was called chain lace in England and crochet lace in France. In 1916, Guiana Indians' descendants were visited by Walter Edmund Roth, where he found examples of crochet.

Lis Paludan, a writer and researcher from Denmark, had three theories. She said that crochet might have originated in Arabia, then spread westwards to Spain and eastward to Tibet, eventually making its way to Mediterranean countries. She also said that crochet's earliest evidence was found in South America, in which a primitive tribe was claimed to have used crochet adornments during puberty rites. Her third theory states that early forms of crochet, particularly three-dimensional dolls, were found in China.

Paludan added that there isn't any convincing evidence about how old crochet may be or where it really originated. It was not possible to look for evidence in Europe before the 1800s. A lot of sources also claimed that crochet has already been known as far back as the 1500s. It was called nun's lace or nun's work in Italy because it was used by nuns for church textiles.

Another theory was that crochet was directly developed from Chinese needlework, which is an ancient form of embroidery known in India, Turkey, North Africa, and Persia and has reached Europe in the 1700s. It was actually called the tambourine, which came from tambour, the French word for drum. In this method, a frame is used to stretch the background fabric while the working thread is held beneath it. A hook with a needle is inserted, and a loop is drawn through the fabric. While the loop is still on the hook, the hook is inserted farther along with the fabric, and another loop is drawn up to form a chain stitch. Tambour hooks are as thin as needles, which is why a very fine thread has to be used.

In Europe, crocheting began to grow in the early nineteenth century, and at that point, it was known as 'shepherd's knitting.' People found this name befitting because crochet seemed like a cheap alternative to purchasing expensive cloth and lace. With the rule of Queen Victoria, crocheting was made popular thanks to her, as she was found purchasing Irish lace crochet items from the people of Ireland during the potato famine. Queen Victoria also picked up crocheting herself, which popularized the craft throughout England.

Crochet is not only historical in this sense, but it was also a lifesaver. Many poor families were pulled out of starvation because of the potato famine, which lasted for five years, by crocheting. They sold their crochet work to well-off people

abroad. During this time, they had a hard time w
living. So, they crocheted in the day in between chore
sun has set, they use candlelight to see their crochet

However, keeping their crochet projects had been quite a
problem, for most of them were living in squalor. They did not
have a place to store their work. Keeping their crochet projects
under their bed only made them dirty. Good thing, these things
could be washed. However, most of the buyers from other
countries were not aware that their delicate cuffs and collars were
made in poor condition.

The Irish workers, including children, men, and women, were
organized into cooperatives. They formed schools to teach
individuals how to crochet. They also trained teachers and sent
them to different parts of Ireland, so they can teach more people
how to crochet. Soon enough, the workers were able to design
and create their own crochet patterns. Even though a lot of
people died in less than ten years, they were still able to survive
the potato famine. More than one million Irish citizens perished,
but many families were still able to make it through, thanks to
their crochet projects. The money they made from selling crochet
work allowed them to save up and immigrate to other countries.
A lot of them actually went to America.

In the 1900s, Irish folks landed in the US, bringing with them
their crocheting skills. It was believed that two million Irish

people went to America between 1845 and 1859, and four million more went there by 1900.

The American women were busy with weaving, spinning, quilting, and knitting back then, but they were still influenced by the Irish to crochet. This explains why the Americans have also become adept at crocheting.

The Evolution of Crochet

In the early centuries, it was the men's job to create their handiwork. Fishermen and hunters, for instance, created knotted strands of cords, strips of cloth, or woven fibers to snare birds or fish and trap animals. They also made fishing nets, knotted game bags, and cooking utensils. They created things that have practical uses.

Eventually, they expanded their handiwork to personal decors. They used these things during special occasions, such as celebrations, religious rites, marriages, and funerals. It was common to see ceremonial costumes that featured crochet-like ornamentation as well as decorative trimmings for the wrists, arms, and ankles.

During the 16th century, wealthy people and members of the royal family of Europe wore jackets, gowns, headpieces, and lace-trimmings. The poor people cannot afford such lavish clothing;

hence, they used crochet to make their clothing more attractive. Crochet became their imitation of expensive lace.

Fast forward to the Victorian era; crochet patterns were made for birdcage covers, flower pot holders, card baskets, lampshades, lamp mats, tablecloths, wastepaper baskets, tobacco pouches, antimacassars, purses, caps, waistcoats, and rugs with foot warmers.

From 1900 until 1930, the women became busy crocheting slumber rugs, Afghans, traveling rugs, sleigh rugs, chaise lounge rugs, car rugs, coffee cozies, teapot cozies, hot water bottle covers, and cushions. During this time, potholders were popularized and became a staple in every repertoire.

During the war in the 1950s, crocheting was used for making items such as under-helmet caps and nets for soldiers. It was also used by women to embellish dresses and hats, particularly when they did not have access to money and resources. During the 1960s, it was all the rage for women to have crochet fabric, and they began crocheting their pantsuits and shift dresses.

The rise of crocheting rose in popularity in the 1970s as granny squares made their debut in dresses, jackets, and hooded sweatshirts that were made entirely out of these motifs. Next came the 1980s, and there was a full-blown rise in crochet-use in fashion, from crochet cardigans to fete style toys. Sometime in the 1990s, crocheting dwindled, but with the internet, Instagram, and other social media platforms, crocheting is back with a modern makeover for all things stylish, from kid's toys to home accessories, to clothing items for both women and men.

Chapter 2: Let's Start Here

When we think of crocheting, most of us imagine a nice lace shawl or something similar made from lace or yarn of some kind, whether it be wool, acrylic, or cotton. But these are not the only materials that you can use in crochet. Below are some other types of materials you can use to crochet that perhaps you have not considered until now.

Fabric Crochet is not a new technique; it has been around since at least the 1800s. There were actual patterns of rag rug available in the 1910s, 20s, and 30s. The downside to working with fabrics is that it can be much more strenuous on your arms and fingers. It is easier to work with thread and wool, but you will save money and do some refurbishing by doing fabric crochet. Make sure that you allow yourself plenty of time to finish a fabric crochet project so that you can well rest your hands between sessions of your project.

As a beginner, you have to choose an easy crochet pattern, but also one that's fun to work with. Once you are comfortable with your skills, you can upgrade to more advanced patterns. As a beginner, you need to take small steps and enjoy the crocheting process instead of becoming overwhelmed with an advanced pattern and getting discouraged. This might cause you to give up on your crocheting journey altogether. There are plenty of beautiful crochet patterns to try for beginners. One way to identify what would work best for you is to look at the crochet pattern schematic.

Understanding the Crochet Pattern

When you have chosen a pattern, the next thing to do is to read the instructions completely, which also includes the stitch guide, any notes that come with it, the diagrams, charts, and the finishing sections. Confusion can be avoided by reading these notes. You will also find plenty of information on tips and techniques, construction guidelines for keeping track of your stitches, as well as what to do with scrap yarn. As a beginner, you will seek immense knowledge by going through the stitch guide and identifying the kinds of stitches that you have never tried before.

Gauge Swatch

The gauge swatch is very important for beginners, although it is often considered the least interesting part of crocheting. Despite its unpopular reputation, the gauge swatch will help you determine the size of your final product.

The gauge swatch is important, especially if you are substituting yarn with others having the same size or weight. When you use substituted yarn, along with the individual crochet tension that goes with it, you may not always end up with the exact gauge with your hook size. If you end up with a wrong or different gauge size, try using a smaller or larger hook depending on your project. This tiny step can make a huge difference to your overall project.

Substituting Yarn in Crochet Patterns

When you do decide to substitute the yarn specified in your pattern, you would need to look for the correct yarn size. If your pattern calls for worsted weight yarn, then look for another type of worsted weight yarn. This does not mean that your yarn size will be correct, but it may require you to play around with different hook sizes to get the right gauge.

Wraps per inch are the best indicator of correct yarn size substitute. Wraps per inch or (wpi) can be found by wrapping the yarn continuously around a ruler and then counting the number of wraps you can make in an inch. Keep the fiber content in mind when you substitute yarn. Silk and cotton often have different drapes compared to animal fiber such as wool or alpaca. Pure silk and cotton also stretch, and they can 'grow' over time. You can also use acrylic blends or even acrylic yarn as alternatives to animal or plant fibers.

A final note to any beginner is to always believe in your pattern. Anyone attempting this for the first time is bound to hit many road bumps and dead ends, and it is the same for you and your crocheting.

9 Tips to Get You Started

1. Learn all you can about crochet supplies so you can purchase what suits you.

2. Remove all obstacles in your way. This can be your long hair, jewelry, and cats (because they cannot resist a ball of yarn!), so you aren't interrupted while you work.

3. Position the yarn in a place that unwinds easily.

4. Be prepared to switch hooks. Novice crocheters often work too tight or too loose. If this is the case for you, change your hook. (Too tight = a larger hook needed; too loose = a smaller hook needed).

5. Take the time to make gauge swatches, practice all the stitches that you'll need for a pattern.

6. Don't be afraid to experiment with making a project your own. If you make a mistake, you can always unravel the last few stitches.

7. Take a break. If you get frustrated, taking a breather can help you refocus when you come back to work. A break is also good for hand and finger stretching. You don't want to injure yourself as you work, or you might never get to finish your project.

8. Keep up-to-date with everything crochet. There are plenty of online e-zines and forums filled with all of the latest patterns, tips, tricks, and information. You never know what you'll learn!

9. Of course, the best way to master crochet is through practice. After all, practice makes perfect!

Chapter 3: Types of Crochet

When we talk about yarn, most people assume it is only meant for knitting. Not to mention, many people think knitting and crocheting are the same. Knitting and crocheting have the same distinctions, especially when it comes to the tools needed to crochet.

Crocheting has its very own finishes, tools, and techniques, and none of this can be achieved through knitting.

As beginners, it is also good to know the different types of crochet that exists in our world. Take note that crocheting was not a thing in Europe or America. Different variations existed in different parts of the world to be used for a variety of uses, from bags to traditional headgear, clothing, bracelets, adornments, as well as home decor.

Here is a list of 21 well-known crocheting types that still exist in the world and are being practiced everywhere:

1. Amigurumi Crochet

This is the most popular form of crochet, and its country of origin is Japan. Amigurumi refers to the art of creating small, stuffed toys or objects from crocheted yarn. Amigurumi means to crochet or even to knit, whereas nuigurumi refers to stuffed dolls. Whenever you see a doll or toy made of yarn, it is most likely amigurumi. Many popular culture items have been used to make amigurumi, such as Hello Kitty, Mario Brothers, Pokemon, and Winnie the Pooh.

2. Aran Crochet

This type of crochet is usually cabled or ribbed. It has its roots in Celtic culture and features interlocking cables. It is often the choice of crochet used for making bigger items such as scarves, sweaters, and beanies. If you see the word 'Aran' in your patterns, be careful because Aran is also used to describe the weight of yarn. Cozy blankets and throws are usually made using Aran crochet.

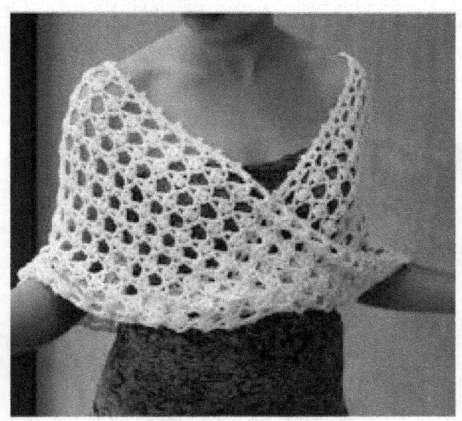

Items made using Aran crochet:

- Blankets
- Jackets
- Coats
- Scarves
- Throws

3. Bavarian crochet

This Bavarian type of crochet is a vintage crochet stitch, and it is traditionally used in rounds. The resulting piece is often a thick fabric that procures for smooth and blended color changes compared to sharp color changes such as the ones commonly seen in a granny square. With Bavarian crochet, you will work in two parts. The first part is the base of clusters, whereas the second part is followed by a row of shells. The Bavarian crochet is the fancier cousin to the granny square.

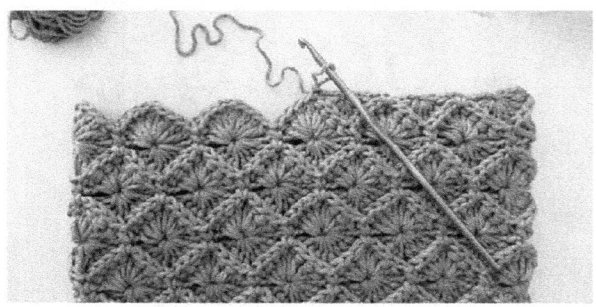

Items made using Bavarian crochet:

- Blankets
- Shawls
- Tabletop covers

4. Bosnian Crochet

This type of crochet has a knit-like fabric and is quite dense. It is crocheted using a slip stitch and crocheted in different parts from the row before. Bosnian crochet also uses a different type of hook, conveniently called Bosnian crochet hook, which you can buy, but using regular hooks can work just as well. This type of crochet is called Shepherd's knitting since it also looks like knitted fabrics.

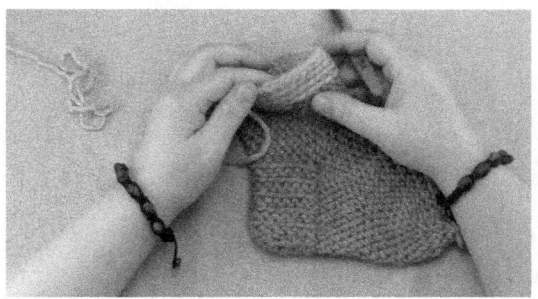

Items made using Bosnian crochet:

- Scarves
- Beanies
- Socks
- Hand gloves

5. Bullion Crochet

This crochet is a specialized stitch and is achieved using a combination of multiple yarn wraps on a long crochet hook. The result is a distinctive roll stitch, which appears unique too. Motifs are usually made using bullion crochet, and it results in a uniform, thick, and round motif style piece.

Items made using Bullion crochet:

- Stiff items such as placemats
- Motifs for decoration

6. Broomstick Crochet

Also known as jiffy lace, broomstick crochet is a type of vintage crochet stitch, which is made with a traditional crochet hook. The resulting stitches are formed around a long and wide object such as a broomstick handle, which is how it gets its name. Modern people who crochet use larger crochet hooks or even thick dowels when doing broomstick crochet. This type of crochet is an excellent skill to learn and master as its final product is very beautiful and unique.

Items made using Broomstick crochet:

- Delicate shawls
- Throw blankets for decoration

7. Bruges Crochet

Ribbons of crochet can be created using this type. These ribbons are then crocheted together, and the results show an intricate lace pattern. This is also the most common type of crochet used in home decor items.

Items made using Bruges crochet:

- Intricate shawls
- Embellishments for clothing
- Tablecloths

8. Clothesline Crochet

In this crochet style, traditional crochet stitches are done over a clothesline or thick rope or even thick twine to make baskets and circular mats to hold their shape. This type of crocheting can be traced back to Africa and Nepal.

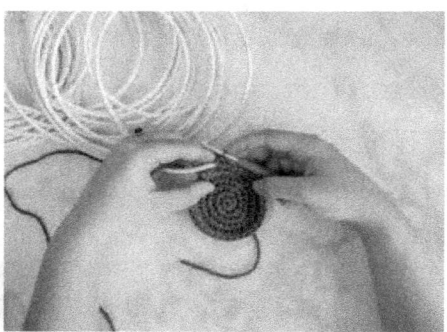

Items made using clothesline crochet:

- Baskets
- Mats
- Structural wall hanging

9. Clones Lace Crochet

This type of crochet is associated with Irish lace crochet. It was created to be an alternative to the Irish lace crochet because it's easier and quicker to make than the Irish needlepoint lace. The clones knot used for this type of crocheting requires a unique crochet skillset. Clones lace is a very practical crochet style, and it was commonly used during wars since it was quick and fast to make.

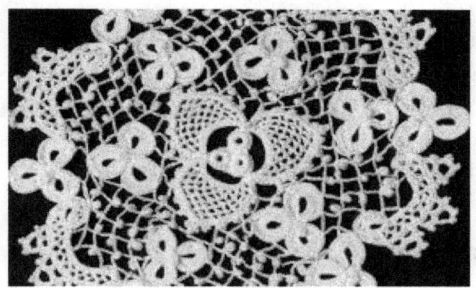

Items made using clones lace crochet:

- Open weave scarves
- Delicate dresses and tops

10. Cro-hook Crochet

This uniquely named crochet is created using a double-ended hook to create double-sided crochet. This enables you to make stitches in or out at either end of the crochet piece, and this piece does not have a wrong or right side to work on. Because of its nature, this type of crochet is called the Cro-hook or the Cro-knit. This type of crochet closely resembles Tunisian crochet and is an excellent option if you're working with colors that aren't manageable with other types of crochet.

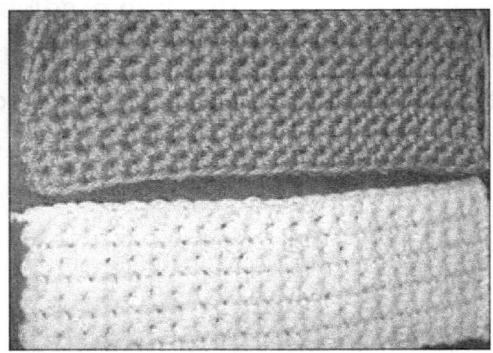

Items made using cro-hook crochet:

- Washcloths
- Scarves
- Baby blankets

11. Filet Crochet

This style is created using chain rows and double crochet stitches. What you get is a grid-like pattern wherein the squares are either filled or not filled, and the negative space is usually there to create images with the pieces. The wonderful thing about this type of crochet is that you can be completely creative and embed images using empty or full squares of fabric.

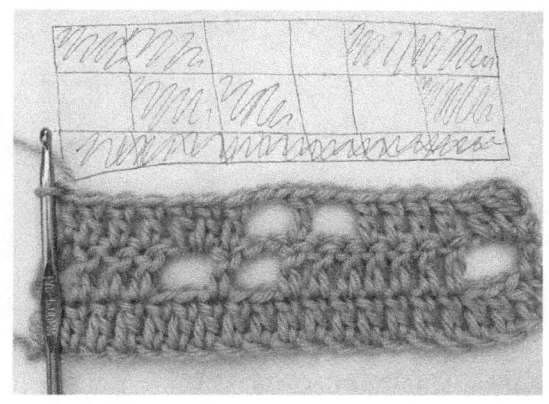

Items made using filet crochet:

- Baby blankets
- Jackets and kimonos
- Handbags
- Cushions

12. Finger Crochet

This type of crochet is called as such because it does not require hooks. It is similar to finger knitting. It's basically hand fabric that you can use to weave crochet stitches. This is a fun crochet to do when you are a beginner, but the resulting piece has loose tension, which is probably why people move on to hooks to make more versatile projects.

Items made using finger crochet:

- Simple string bags
- Basic scarves

13. Freeform Crochet

This type of crochet is called freeform because there is no pattern or plan to follow. It is entirely up to the person crocheting to create something. This type of crochet is very artistic and organic, making it an excellent option for beginners. However, if you find yourself struggling without instructions or even a plan, then it's best to avoid freeform and follow crochet pieces with patterns.

Items made using freeform crochet:

- One-off clothing items
- Art pieces

14. Hairpin Crochet

Like the broomstick crochet, the hairpin crochet is made using the traditional crochet hook, but instead of a broomstick, the piece is held taut using thin metal rods. In earlier times, this technique used actual hairpins, which is how it got its name. The resulting piece is unique and beautiful.

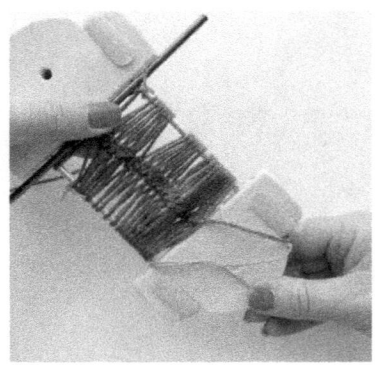

Items made using hairpin crochet:

- Delicate scarves
- Shawls
- Wraps

15. Micro Crochet

Micro crochet is a modern crochet style and is made using very fine yarn thread with extremely fine or small crochet hooks. It is a very delicate crocheting process and is great for those who are patient and like dainty and small things.

Item made using micro crochet:

- Tiny things for dollhouses
- Embellishments
- Talisman

16. Overlay Crochet

This technique is also unique where a base of crochet stitches is made, and then other stitches are added to the top to create a raised pattern. This crocheting technique is more advanced, and it brings many possibilities for you to create intricate pieces.

Items made using overlay crochet:

- Potholders
- Wall hangings
- Handbags

17. Pineapple Crochet

The pineapple crochet is considered more of a general stitch and shape rather than a technique. You can use this crochet to create scarves, doilies, and certain types of clothing. This stitch was very popular in the 1970s, and once you know how to spot this type of stitch, you will be seeing it everywhere.

Items made using pineapple crochet:

- Dresses
- Tops
- Shawls
- Wraps

18. Stained Glass Crochet

The stained-glass crochet could be mistaken for the overlay crochet. However, it is different because the top part is normally made using only black yarn to accentuate the colors and create a stained-glass effect. What you get is a very striking crochet pattern.

Items made using stained glass crochet:

- Thick, sturdy items
- Winter scarves
- Handbags

19. Symbol Crochet

The symbol crochet is another type of popular crochet and is the favorite among the Japanese. It is also known as the "chart" crochet and is another one of those crochet skills that are crucial to learning because you can make any projects from any crochet books in any language and create them all by looking at a chart.

Items made using symbol crochet:

- Complicated patterns that are difficult to explain in words
- Intricate designs
- Motifs
- Foreign language patterns

20. Tapestry Crochet

As the name goes, plenty of color goes into creating this piece, and it is also known as "intarsia" crochet. Tapestry crochet is used in many different parts of the world, and it also has many different methods, which result in a variety of styles. If you want to do color work, using tapestry crochet enables you to create intricate patterns with a variety of colored yarn.

Items made using tapestry crochet:

- Color workpieces
- Imagery based designs

21. Tunisian Crochet

This type of crochet is done on a long hook that has a stopper at the end. When you look at Tunisian crochet, it can be very similar to knitting because of the many live loops, and you need to work your loops on and off your hook, similar to knitting.

Items made using tapestry crochet:

- Knit-look items
- Blankets
- Scarves

Chapter 4: Materials Needed for Crochet

Fiber type

This is the first decision you have to make as you embark on your crochet journey. There are several options to choose from for both plant and animal fibers. However, we will focus on the three most common and basic ones: acrylic, cotton, and wool.

You might be wondering how to know which type of fiber you are working with, but it's really quite simple—the type of fiber is usually listed on the yarn label. Although, as you familiarize yourself with crocheting, you will find yourself being able to identify the fiber type by just handling or even looking at the yarn.

Yarn

You can use a variety of yarns to crochet, but the type of yarn you chose depends on the type of project. You can crochet with any kind of yarn, even with non-fiber materials. While you can use any type of yarn, as a beginner, you will find it best to use the yarn options we will outline below since they are easier to work with than others.

Choosing the Best Yarn for Crochet

Acrylic yarn: Acrylic is generally a popular yarn among crochet enthusiasts. It is usually among the affordable choices for yarn, comes in a variety of colors, and is widely available. It is a more than acceptable choice for you as a beginner. However, you should be aware that some of the cheapest acrylics split apart, thereby making it quite challenging to work with. This case is not usually common, but it does happen. Therefore, if you are having a hard time working with acrylic, try switching to a different brand, or you can just use wool or cotton instead.

Cotton yarn: It's an inelastic fiber, thereby making it a bit more challenging to work with than wool. However, where you want the item to hold its shape, this quality makes cotton a great choice for specific projects. Although some may find it a bit more challenging than wool, it is not that different at all, and it is something you can certainly try as a beginner. If you are crocheting during summer, where working with wool is unpleasant due to the heat, cotton is a great choice since it's lighter than wool.

Wool yarn: Wool is the perfect choice for you to practice your stitches. It forgives mistakes and is a resilient fiber. If you happen to make a mistake while crocheting, most wool yarns are easy to unravel and even re-use (in crochet, it's called frogging). Wool yarn is not suitable for those with wool allergies, but for most, it is a good crocheting choice.

Additional Yarn Tips and Considerations

Yarn weight: Yarns come in different thicknesses as well. This thickness is what we refer to as weight. The weight of the yarn is usually found on the label, where it's numbered 1–7 (from the thinnest to the thickest). It is easiest to work with a worsted weight yarn as a beginner, which is #4 on the yarn label.

*Note: you should use the correct crochet hook size for the yarn weight you will be using.

Yarn color: Choose lighter yarn colors rather than dark ones, as it can get challenging to see your stitches if using yarns with dark colors.

Yarn texture: Choose smooth yarn and not textured ones. As you begin crocheting, avoid eyelash yarns and any other textured novelty yarns, which can get quite frustrating to work with.

Yarn yardage: Each ball of yarn has different yardage amounts, which relates to the price. You can find two balls of yarn at the same price; just check the yardage to ensure the amount of yarn in each ball is approximately the same.

Yarn price: The price of yarn varies significantly from brand to brand and fiber to fiber. It is better to work on the affordable ones so that you get the hang of it before investing a lot of money in very expensive yarns. This is why acrylic, wool, and cotton are the top fiber choices, as they tend to be the most affordable.

Yarn color dye lot: If you want to crochet a large project that will need more than one ball of yarn, then you want to ensure that all the colors match (assuming that you are using the same color-way or color for the entire project). You do this by checking the dye lot on the yarn label to ensure that the balls are from the same dye lot number so that they don't have noticeable differences between them.

Washing details: Different fiber types have different washing instructions, which will be really important if you are crocheting something to wear. For instance, you can use superwash wool that is safe to put in the washer and dryer, or you can do so for some type of wool that must be hand washed and dried flat because it will shrink in the dryer. The yarn label contains this information to aid in your selections.

Hooks

The average crochet hook works for anyone, and it definitely favors beginners like you. You will find crochet hooks sold at yarn stores or any major craft retailer. You can also get them online. Below are a few things you need to know about crochet hooks:

Material

A basic crochet hook can be made of several common materials such as bamboo, plastic, and aluminum. Most people usually choose aluminum crochet hooks for their first project. There are also fancier crochet hooks made of wood, glass, and clay.

Size

Crochet hooks differ in size; many different sizes are measured in numbers, letters, or millimeters. For instance, a basic crochet hook set may range from E–J. A general-sized crochet hook is normally H-8 5mm. Size E is smaller than size H; size J is larger. You should match the size of your crochet hook with the weight of your yarn, which is usually on the label of the yarn. For most beginners, it is usually advisable to work with a size G or H crochet hook and worsted weight yarn. Since neither is better than the other, if you find it hard to work with one, just try the other.

Types of Crochet Hooks

Let us now look at the various types of crochet hooks at your disposal as you get started:

Hook throat: a crochet hook has either an inline or tapered "throat," resulting in less or more flatness to the head of the hook.

Thread Crochet Hooks: when you are using thread to crochet instead of yarn, the crochet hook you use is similar, but it is quite smaller than a yarn hook. The hooks are also usually made of steel to prevent bending while you crochet, a problem that is less popular among larger hook sizes.

Light-up crochet hooks: if you suffer from insomnia or you simply want to crochet in the middle of the night without being a bother to anyone, then light-up crochet hooks are what you need.

They light up at the tip so that it is easier to see where you are going to insert the hook to crochet. These are usually regular crochet hooks that light up.

Ergonomic crochet hooks: sometimes, it can become quite uncomfortable to crochet with regular hooks for a long time, especially if you suffer from hand conditions such as arthritis or carpal tunnel. Fortunately, there are ergonomic crochet hooks, which have larger handles that are shaped to create a grip that makes it easier to crochet for long.

Tunisian crochet hooks: Tunisian crochet is a niche of crocheting that uses a completely different set of stitches from regular crocheting. Tunisian crochet hooks are also known as Afghan crochet hooks and are longer than the regular crochet hooks. These hooks can have a cable to connect a one-headed hook to another, or they can have a head on each side of the hook.

Knook: A knook looks like a regular crochet hook, but it has a small hole drilled into one end where you insert the thread for holding your stitches.

CROCHET HOOK CONVERSATION CHART

METRIC	US	UK
2.00	-	14
2.25	B/1	13
2.50	-	12
2.75	C/2	11
3.00	-	11
3.25	D/3	10
3.50	E/4	9
3.75	F/5	-
4.00	G/6	8
4.50	-	7
5.00	H/8	6
5.50	I/9	5

6.00	J/10	4
6.5	K/10,5	3
7.00	-	2
8.00	L/11	0
9.00	M/13	00
10.00	N/15	000
11.50	P/16	-
15.75/16.00	Q	-

Chapter 5: How to Read and Understand Crochet

How to Read the Pattern

One of the most important things in crochet is knowing how to read the pattern.

At the beginning of your experience, it is important to find models at an appropriate skill level, based on the difficulty level to understand if you are able to complete the job. To do this, ask yourself two questions:

- Do you know the points you will need to use?
- Can you follow the instructions?

Once you have found the model, it is important to see all the symbols and abbreviations included in it to understand if the job is within your reach.

American and English patterns are typically written while in Japan or other countries, it will be drawn. The latter, rather than using words, uses a pictorial diagram like the one shown below.

If you are a knitter, you are probably familiar with scheduled work; however, crochet charts are drawn rather than graphed.

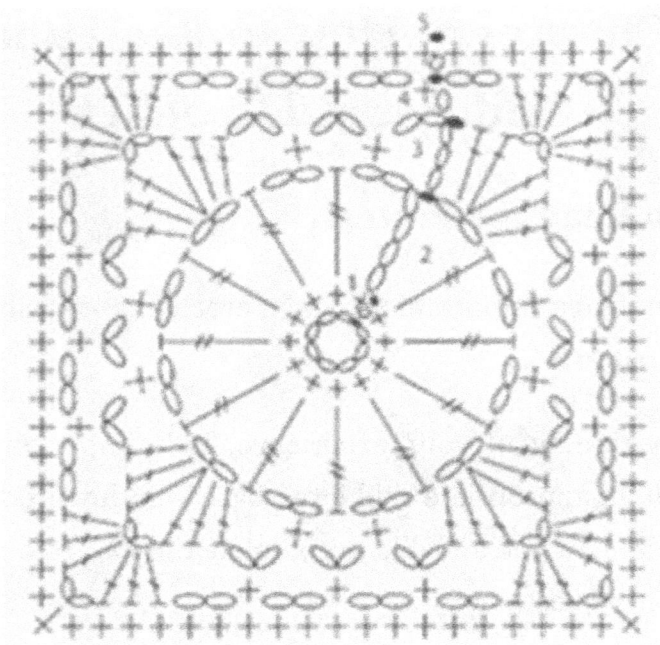

Crochet charts are used for a variety of different projects and can, with a bit of practice, be more practical and effective than written instructions. Today, more designers are opting for charts or are including both charts and written instructions.

For a complex chart, you may want to also use a row counter. A row counter allows you to click or move a bead to track how many rows you've completed. While this isn't typically necessary for a small chart, it can be very helpful for larger charts.

Most patterns begin with a series of loops, also called chains or a slip stitch. Nevertheless, you can easily learn how to create a foundation without using a standard chain. Projects are typically worked in rows wherein you have to switch back and forth, with every row over the previous row. You can also stitch in rounds wherein you work around a ring of chains and create a geometric figure, such as a circle, hexagon, or square. You can also use a motif or a geometric piece to stitch together and form your crochet project.

As already said before, you'll find stitch patterns written in two different ways.

The first is the most typical and will be found in vintage patterns, as well as many modern American and British patterns. This is a fully written out stitch pattern, using typical and traditional stitch notation.

Some modern designers in the west, as well as Japanese crochet patterns, do not rely upon written out notation but on a graphic representation of crochet stitches. These look nothing at all like craft charts you might have used, like those for cross-stitching or knitting. They are, in fact, rather pictorial, with picture symbols written out for each round or row. Once you're used to reading crochet charts, you'll find you can do so with relative ease.

- Charts are much more commonly used for doilies or shawls, rather than simple projects, like a hat or afghan.
- Charts are rarely used for repeated stitch patterns but can be.

Written crochet patterns are still the most common in America and Britain. They are relatively easy to use, and pattern notation is largely standardized.

An example of a written model is the following: make a chain of any length desired, plus 3 stitches for turning.

- **Row 1:** Make 5 DC in the 3rd st from the end, * skip 2 ch, make 1 SC in next stitch, skip 2 and make 5 DC in next stitch. *
- **Row 2.** Ch. 3, and turn. Work 4 DC into SC * 1 SC into 3rd DC of the previous row, 5 DC into SC of the previous row. Repeat from * across row.
- Repeat Row 2 to the desired length.

Let's take a longer look at this in a written-out form:

- **Row 1:** Make 5 double crochet stitches in the third stitch from the end of the chain. *Skip 2 chains, make one, the crochet should be single the next stitch, skip 2 chains and make 5 double crochet stitches in the next stitch.*
- **Row 2:** Chain 3 and turn. Work 4 double crochet into single crochet. Work one the crochet should be single to 3rd double crochet of the previous row, 5 double crochet into the single crochet of the previous row.
- Repeat from * to end.

With just a little practice, the abbreviations will become second nature.

Note: If you're an American and using a British pattern, or you're British and using an American pattern, there's a bit of a quirk between the two languages.

British Notation	American Notation
double crochet (dc)	single crochet (sc)
half treble (htr)	half double crochet (hdc)
treble (tr)	double crochet (dc)
double treble (dtr)	treble (tr)
triple treble (trtr)	double treble (dtr)
miss	skip
tension	gauge
yarn over hook (yoh)	yarn over (yo)

Do you see the difference? The UK doesn't use the term single crochet; single crochet is called a double, and double crochet is called a treble. The treble crochet is called a double treble. Reviewing the pattern key can help you to know whether you're working with a British or American pattern, but it's an easy adjustment, especially as you get used to working the pattern.

An example of a model based on the Pythagorean diagram is the following:

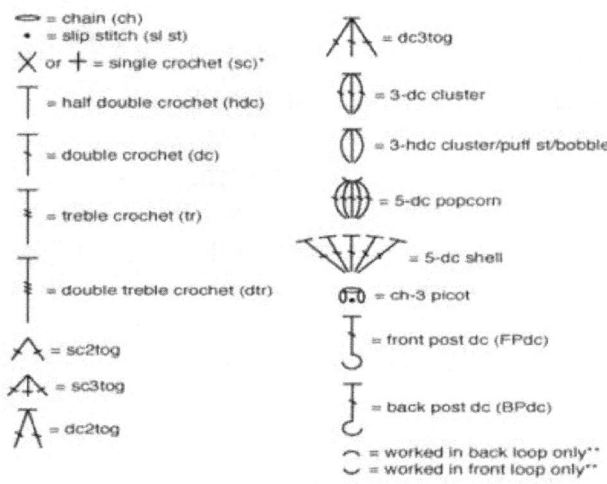

The key above illustrates crochet chart symbols. The symbols themselves are universal but do notice that the language refers to American crochet notation and work the stitches accordingly.

When assembled to form a chart, the symbols might look like:

You may notice something about this chart right away. It creates a visual very similar to the finished work, making it easy to realize that your project should look like, even if you don't have a picture of the finished work.

- **Round 1:** Ch 16, join with a sl st.
- **Round 2:** Ch 3, work one dc in the first chain of the previous round. *work one dc in next stitch, 2 dc in next around* join with a sl st. (24)
- **Round 3:** Ch 3, sk 1 dc, sc in next, *ch 3, sk 1 dc, SC in next* join with a sl st.

- **Round 4:** Ch 3, *1 dc in first sc, sk 1 ch, *10 dc in 2nd ch stitch, sk 1 ch, 1 SC in sc* to last ch 3 loops. 9 dc in 2nd ch st, sl st to join to 3rd ch in initial ch 3.
- **Round 5:** Sc in 6th dc of last dc cluster, ch 5, dc in sc of prev round, ch5, *sc in 6th dc of the cluster, ch10, dc in sc of prev round, ch 5, dc in sc of prev round, ch5* join with sl st.
- **Round 6:** Working backward to reverse direction, slip stitch in the first 5 ch stitches to the left of your hook. This returns you to the corner of your work. Ch 8, sc in the third ch of ch 5 of the previous round. *Ch 5 sc in the third ch of ch 5 of the previous round. Ch5, dc 3 in 6th ch of ch 10 of prev round, ch 3, dc3 in the same space*. On the last repeat, dc 2, using the first 3 chains of initial chain 8 to make the third dc. Join with sl st at the third chain.
- **Round 7:** Working backward again, sl st in the first 5 stitches to reach the corner of your work. Ch 8, sc in the third ch of ch 5 of the previous round. *Ch 5 sc in the third ch of ch 5 of the previous round. Ch5, sc in the third ch of ch 5 of prev round, dc 3 in 6th ch of ch 10 of prev round, ch 3, dc3 in same space*. On the last repeat, dc 2, using the first 3 chains of initial chain 8 to make the third dc. Join with sl st at the third chain.
- **Round 8:** Working backward again, sl st in the first 5 stitches to reach the corner of your work. Ch 8, sc in the third ch of ch 5 of the previous round. *Ch 5 sc in the third

ch of ch 5 of the previous round. Ch5, sc in the third ch of ch 5 of prev round, Ch5, sc in the third ch of ch 5 of prev round, dc 3 in 6th ch of ch 10 of prev round, ch 3, dc3 in same space*. On the last repeat, dc 2, using the first 3 chains of initial chain 8 to make the third dc. Join with sl st at a third chain.

Note: Rounds 6, 7, and 8 are nearly identical, with the addition of one more ch5 loop per side in each round.

As you can see, that's a very cumbersome pattern written out. It's much easier to follow and understand working from a pictorial chart. This is the benefit of charts for complex and lacy work. If you'd like, you can even make your charts, either by hand or using online charting software.

Crochet Terms and Abbreviations

Alt = alternate

Beg = means beginning, as the beginning of the row

Bp = means "back post" like rather than working through the loops, you are working the stitch around the post. You typically pair it with the abbreviation of the stitch you are using. For example, bpdc stands for back post double crochet whereas bpsc stands for back post single crochet

BL = refers to the "back loop" crochet. It might also be seen as BLO "back loop only." Occasionally BL can also be used to refer to bobbles or blocks, specific to the pattern using it. For this information, check the stitch list of the pattern that is usually found at the beginning of the pattern

BO = bobble

Cl = cluster. Your pattern should specify the type of cluster being used, as there are many different types of clusters. For instance, 3 tr cluster refers to a cluster of 3 treble crochet stitches

Ch(s) = chain(s). This is one of the most common abbreviations you will see since almost all crochet patterns start with chains. Most patterns also include chains throughout the design.

Dtr = double treble crochet

Dec = decrease. It's a technique used for shaping in crochet

Dc = double crochet. It's one among the most common basic crocheting stitches

Incl = inclusive/including/include

Inc = increase. It's another technique used in shaping, like dec (decreasing) is used

Hdc or **half dc** = half double crochet. It's a basic crochet stitch in between double crochet and single crochet in height

Fp = front post, as compared to "back post" explained above

FL = front loop. It is also abbreviated as FLO (front loop only) in contrast to BL/BLO as earlier mentioned

Oz = ounce(s). It's likely to be seen in the part of the patterns of crocheting, explaining how much yarn is required or on yarn labels. It may also be measured in other ways, such as yards (yd), meters (m), or grams (g)

Pm = place marker

Pc = popcorn. A textured crochet stitch that is similar to bobbles and clusters. Patterns that use these types of stitches normally explain how the designer wants to make the stitch at the beginning of the pattern, where the crochet abbreviation preferred by the designer will also be seen

Rem = remaining

RS = right side. When worked in rows, crochet has both right side and wrong side

Rnd(s) = round(s). They are used for counting when working in the round or otherwise working in circles (in contrast to working in rows)

Rev = reverse. It is typically used together with other abbreviations such as rev sc, which means reverse single crochet stitch

Rep = repeat. It is frequently placed together with symbols that show the part of the pattern that is going to be repeated. Examples:

- [] = the pattern specifies the times to repeat a series of instructions given inside the brackets

- () = the pattern specifies the times to repeat a series of instructions given inside the parentheses

- * = the pattern specifies the times to repeat a series of instructions given between asterisks or following an asterisk

St(s) = stitch(es)

Sp(s) = space (s)

Sl st = slip stitch. It's the method used in joining rounds when crocheting, as well as a stitch that is used on its own

Sk = skip. For instance, you can skip the next chain and work into the one following, which will be indicated by the term sk ch (skip chain)

Sc = single crochet. It is one of the most basic and frequently used crochet stitches

Tr = triple crochet/treble crochet. It's another basic crochet stitch

Tr tr = triple treble crochet. Another tall crochet stitch is even taller than the dtr described earlier

Tog = together. It is sometimes used to replace 'decrease' where it can be written as "sc2tog" to mean a decrease in single crochet stitch

WS = wrong side. It's the opposite of the right side (rs) as earlier described

WIP = work in progress

Yoh = yarn over hook

YO = yarn over. A step used in making most crochet stitches. It's typically not seen in crochet patterns but is often seen in crochet stitch tutorials

approx	approximately
beg	beginning
blo	back loop only
cc	contrast color
ch	chain
cl	cluster
cont	continue
dc	double crochet
dec	decrease
ea	each
gm	grams
gr	group
hdc	half double crochet
hk	hook
inc	increase
incl	including
lp	loop

mc	main color
pat	pattern
rem	remaining
rep	repeat
rnd(s)	round(s)
RS	right side
sc	single crochet
sl	slip
slst	slip stitch
sk	skip
sp	space
st(s)	stitch(es)
tog	together
tr / tc	triple (treble) crochet
WS	wrong side
yo	yarn over

Chapter 6: Basic Crochet Stitches

Basic Crochet stitches

This is a very easy adventure when you enjoy it. The whole process of crocheting begins with a candid and easy-to-understand slipknot. From this, it can graduate into something beautiful both to the eyes as well as pleasing.

Slip Knot

Knowing how to create the slip knot is the first step towards developing your crocheting ability. The slip knot is the basis of most crochet patterns, and therefore, you will need to properly master this so that you can build your ability to choose other trends later.

1. You will begin by laying the thread on a flat surface, then looping once over itself. It should hang down, taking the shape of an inverted U. Here, you will have the tail yarn and working yarn. Tail yarn will be the part that is on the right side, while the working yarn is the end of the string on the left, which is pretty much how crochet begins.

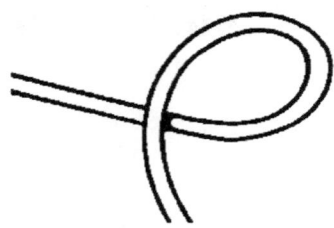

2. Then, loop over with your thread so that the rear part in the wool comes over the one you are working with.

3. Next, once you have done this, run the end of the wool over where they cross and move the loop beneath the working wool.

4. After this, insert the crochet hook through the right side to the left, passing it over the wool you are working with, and then through the cross, you have made.

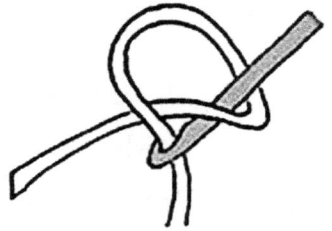

5. Finally, tighten the wool over the hoop. Pull lightly on both ends to tighten it.

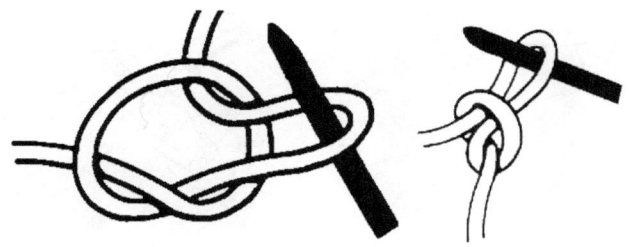

Congratulations, you've just made your first knot.

The Foundation Chain

This is the foundation chain, from which you then begin the crochet. This is also called the chain stitch.

1. After making the slip knot, insert the crochet hook through the right side to the left, as seen before.

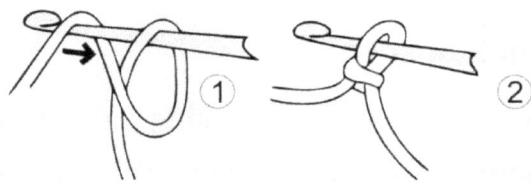

2. Here, hold the hook with the backside downwards while you hold the tail of the string with your other hand, using the finger grip that you are comfortable with. The key is that you maintain it well so that it will be easy for you to make the loops without disrupting the movement of the crochet shaft.

3. Then move it over, with the wool coming to the left side of the hook, then move it to the left side of the first knot.

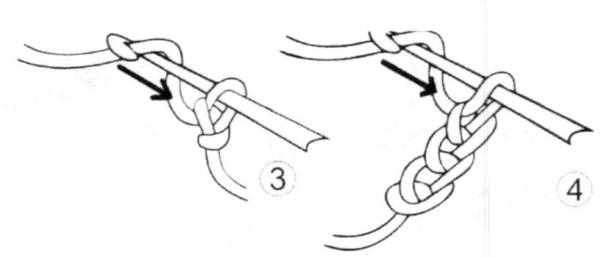

4. Finally, move the working thread through the slip knot, and you will have one loop on the hook and another underneath it. This is your first chain.

Do this over and over, depending on the number of chains that you want to create. So, say you want to create twelve strings, then you will repeat this process over and over twelve times. Do this repeatedly until you can comfortably move the crochet through the working yarn, slip knot, and loops with ease and comfort.

Single Crochet (sc)

This comes to as the third step in making your crochet. This stitch is vital as it is used in so many crochet patterns and is so easy to do. You can do so much with it whether you are working in rows, spirals, or rounds. It is also perfect for edging and combining other stitches. So, let's get to it, shall we?

1. Insert the crochet hook.

2. Once your chain is done, stick your hook in through your first Ch stitch. For the following row, you should put your hook into the single crochet stitch, which lies beneath it in the row, and so on. Slide your hook under both loops, which lie at the top of the chain. (Some patterns work through one loop at a time).

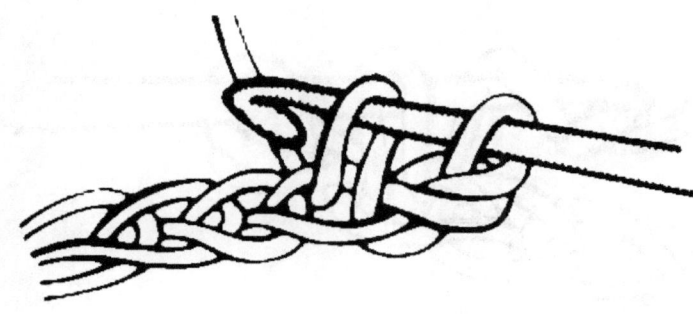

3. When you have done this, move over the working yarn, pulling it to the top side of the crochet hook. Then move the working yarn through the V, bringing the moving wool through the procession you have woven, which will then create two running folds on the hook shaft.

4. Then move it one more time, move the working yarn back through the underside of the hook, passing it through the two loops you have when you do this. You will have one knot on the crochet hook. This is the first crochet that you have made.

To do this, you will need to understand that you will always need to be using the working yarn to make all the loops. That is why it is called the working yarn, after all. Be keen to keep it long then, as you do not want to run out of thread middle of your loop, bringing to a sad end the beautiful artistry that was taking shape.

Once you have completed your first single crochet, then repeat the process through each of the rows of the foundation chain and keep in mind that you will continue using the second V-shaped loops, as this will ensure that you do not have significant unsightly gaps in your knitting.

You will repeat this process for as long as you need, depending on the size of what you are knitting. Then, you move to a third party.

Double Crochet (dc)

The double crochet is another important basic stitch and is one of the foundational stitches, although it can easily be excluded from many simple patterns. You can use this stitch on its own by working rows, or rounds and it is popular in many common stitch patterns such as the granny square, which is a classic, as well as the v-stitch.

These instructions enable you to practice on your own until you are confident with using this stitch.

1. One has to begin with one stitch on their hook, and then they should wrap the yarn over the hook of their needle.
2. Next, insert your hook into the stitch. If you start with a foundation chain, stick your hook into your fourth stitch.

3. You should circle your yarn over the same way that you did it when you inserted your hook the first time. However, now you'll have more yarn on the crochet hook, and it might seem slightly more difficult than it did earlier. It takes time to get it right.

4. There should be three loops left.

5. Repeat yarn over and draw it through.

6. Encircle the yarn over the hook once more and then pass it through the two loops nearest to the end of the hook.

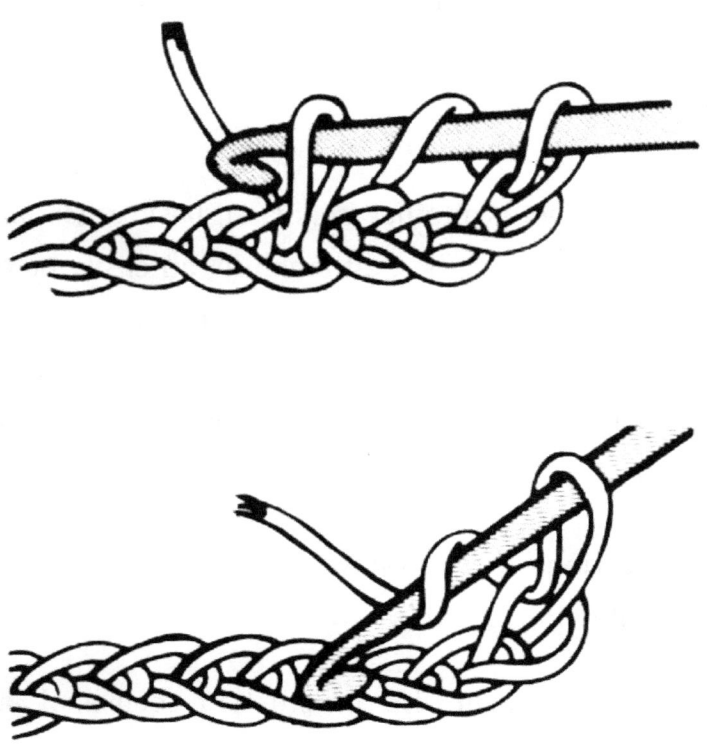

7. Now there are some two loops on the hook.

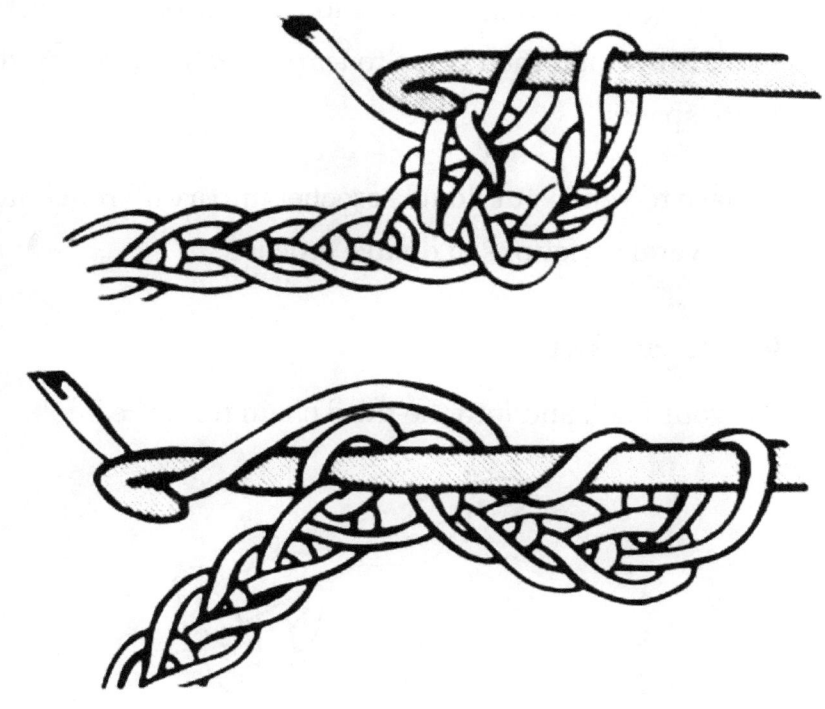

You can build a rhythm as you practice this stitch so that you can yarn over and pass it through your loops; it will seem like one step.

Double crochet hint

The easiest way to practice this stitch is by working it in a straight row. You can stick in the hook to the bottom of these two loops under your own stitch.

For patterns that include spaces, like the granny square, you can do the following: insert your hook into space beneath the stitch you are working rather than into the loops. It is best to practice using regular rows and then go on to learn how to work a double crochet into spaces.

You may have to work your double crochet into a different stitch. There are several variations of double crochet.

Half double crochet

1. YO your hook and into the third chain from the hook.

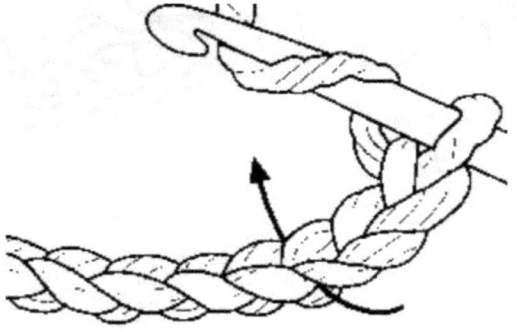

2. Yarn over and into the third chain, and you will have three loops.
3. YO and into the three loops; that is a half double crochet stitch.

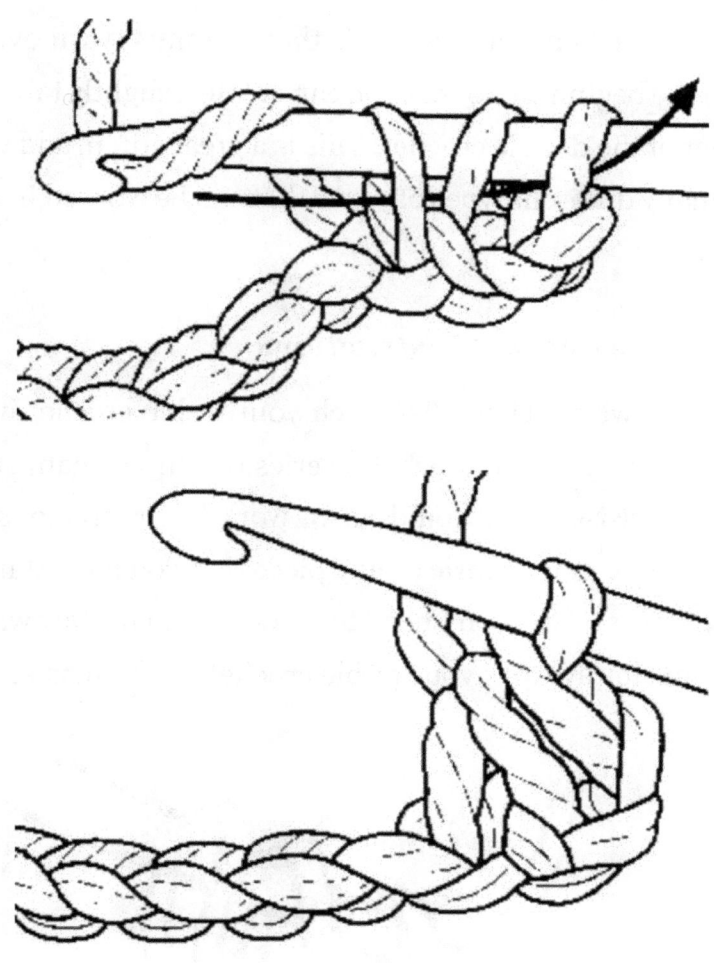

1. YO, insert your hook into the following chain and repeat from step 2.

Treble crochet stitches

This is yet another basic crochet stitch that you can easily master and is fairly similar to the double crochet stitch.

The difference between the two is that you must yarn over once more in the beginning so that you can create a slightly taller stitch than that of the double crochet. This is a great stitch, and you can use so many different types of yarns that can be worked in rounds or rows.

Treble Crochet Instructions

1. Start with a chain. To stitch your treble crochet in rows, you are going to crochet a series of simple chain stitches. Otherwise, you could also work your treble stitches directly into a fabric or any piece that you have started. In that case, you won't need to work a chain to start with; you can simply work your treble crochet on the next stitch.

2. The first four chain stitches on your chain are counted as the first treble stitch. For your next treble stitch, work to your fifth stitch from your hook.

3. To go onto your next treble stitch, encircle your yarn around your crochet hook twice. Now you'll see three loops on the hook, including your working loop that was already there.

4. You have to yarn over the hook and draw it to pass through the two of the loops on your hook. At this point, you have two loops.

5. Again, you have to yarn over and then draw it through both loops on which completes one triple crochet.

6. To continue the row, you should yarn over, then follow by hooking twice, stick your hook into the next chain and proceed to the triple crochet steps given before.

7. To make another row, make four chain stitches, then turn your work. This is what counts as the first triple crochet in the following row, so you'll begin what is known as the triple crochet stitches in the 2nd stitch of the row that came before. To maintain your work very even, you should work the last triple crochet in that row up to the fourth chain of that turning chain from the end of the former row.

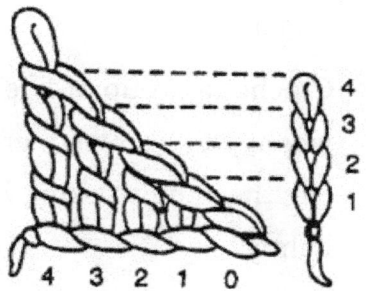

**Insert hook
At Beginning of
Next Row:**

In 1st Stitch
In 1st Stitch
In 2nd Stitch
In 2nd Stitch

4 - Triple Crochet
3 - Double Crochet
2 - Half-Double Crochet
1 - Single Crochet
0 - Slip Stitch

Other Easy Crochet stitches

Popcorn Stitches

For a popcorn mesh, one work—as well as the knobs or flat knobs—a whole group of stitches in a puncture site. The stitches are not taken off together but individually terminated and bundled in a further step. They create plastic accents in even patterns and can be crocheted with fine yarn, as well as with thicker wool qualities.

1. Crochet a group of five rods in a single injection site when you want to crochet a shell. Then slightly lengthen the working loop on the needle by pulling lightly.

2. Now, pull the needle out of the working loop to put it into the debarking element (i.e., the mesh V) of the first stick.

3. Then, pick up the working loop and pull it through the second loop on the needle (the debittering stick of the first stick). Secure the stitch with a chain stitch. Pull the thread through the loop again.

A basic understanding of various knots is possible when seeking to engage in crocheting. Crocheting may be looked at as a subtle adventure, but in the real sense, it is just the way you play with various patterns to create something that pleases the eye. As we have already gathered, crocheting involves the process of changing between the variations of the patterns. The mastery of various patterns of crocheting is achieved through the repetitive process of doing this.

It is key to note that a lot of people can become aware of crocheting just by themselves. Despite this fact, these people still have to use various aids, not limited to photos and tutorials, to achieve this. When seeking help for crocheting, you have a diverse basis on which you can turn to for aid. You should not be limited when seeking to crochet as the patterns that exist are a lot in number, and thus you can choose to settle for what can please you.

When crocheting, you must take note of the hook that you are using because they are of crucial importance. The market has diverse brands of hooks that an individual may choose from when deciding on the process of crocheting. There is a common brand that originates from North America, and there is also that of a founder known as Boyed and Susan Bates. When you compare the hooks of Boyed and that of Bates, you will find that the latter is made up of hooks that are bend in a particular angle that works best when crocheting. This angle is what gives the firm grip to the hook. Hooks vary; your preference may not be the other person's preference. Owing to this fact, you need to settle on a hook that is most comfortable for you. The whole process of crocheting should be enjoyable and not one that takes a toll on you.

Take note of the particular yarn that you use to crochet with. Most amateurs to crocheting go for acrylic yarn. This is because this type of yarn is easily available and can be reliable due to its durability. For amateurs who are seeking to indulge in this venture, there is one that is known as the Super Saver, which can be found in almost every yarn shop in North America. When in the venture, you ought to be cautious enough to inquire from a friend about various things. To do this, you need to ace note of the bitch and the stitch. This involves the various crochet groups that an individual can join to achieve maximum success.

What will help you be a great deal in crocheting is the art of learning to practice while facing the mirror. This act can be helpful a great deal when it comes to the mastery of various patterns that are of great help when it comes to crocheting beautifully. When you crochet while facing the mirror, you are in a position to take note of every move. Once you have achieved this, you are now in a position to master the tutorials through practicing before the mirror. The mirror works as a solid base for checks.

To different people, there are various ways in which an individual may hold his or her yarn. There is one method of holding the yarn that makes it look as if you are holding a pen. This is often referred to as a pen drill. This pen drill is considered traditional because it is one that has been used since time immemorial. There is a different method of holding the yarn that makes it look like you are holding a knife. This type of drill is known as the knife drill. A crocheted may choose one that best suits him. The kind of yarn that a crocheted use is of crucial importance as many experience crocheters have had a hard time too. What has often been adopted is that when the thumb is fuzzier, then it becomes subtle to use.

Tuft Stitches

Basically, tufts are nothing more than inverted shells. They consist of several stitched sewn together; these can be fixed stitches but also double or multiple sticks. Not only do they provide a decorative pattern, but they are also often used to remove one or more stitches in a row.

The base of this tuft is spread over several stitches while their heads are gathered in a stitch. To do this, do not crochet the stitches you want to gather at first to pull the thread through all loops on the needle in the last step. The following instructions for a tuft of three sticks show how to do it exactly.

1. Work the first stick as usual until there are only two loops on the needle. Do the same with the second stick so that you have a total of three loops on the needle.

2. The third stick is also crocheted up to and including the penultimate step. There are four loops on the needle. Now, get the thread.

3. To complete the tufting, pull the thread through all four loops on the needle.

Burl

Knob stitches are very distinctive and give the crochet a beautiful plastic structure. It is a group of several rods or multiple rods, which are worked in the same puncture site and then mixed together, making it a combination of shell and tufts. Pimples are worked in the back row. The following shows how to crochet a knot stitch out of five sticks:

1. Crochet the first stick at the point where you want to create the knit stitch until you have only two loops on the needle.

2. Follow the same procedure for the next four rods working in the same puncture site.

3. Now, there should be a total of six loops on the crochet hook.

4. In the last step, pick up the thread and pull it in one go through all the loops on the needle. It is advisable to secure the knit stitch with a chain stitch (take the

thread and pull it once again through the stitch on the needle) so that the stitches remain firmly together at the top and the knobby effect maintains the desired plasticity.

Tunisian Stitch

The characteristic of the Tunisian stitch is that the picture on the front and back is clearly different. Also, the mice can hardly stretch. Unlike "normal" crocheting, here you have all the hands of a row on the needle. These are summarized in a first step and then mended in a second step. The needle is held like a knitting needle. Choose a crochet hook that is long and has a uniformly thick shaft. You can crochet Tunisian with wool and synthetic yarns.

- **Step 1:** The basis is an air chain, which has to be crocheted loosely. The loops are to be taken, as shown in the picture. You always start at the right edge of the crochet work.

- **Step 2:** In the next step, knit the loop on the left edge with an envelope. After that, two slings are always embarrassed. When the last two loops are cut off, the first row is finished. Many styles of Tunisian crocheting arise with such two steps: grasping and chopping.

- **Step 3:** For the subsequent rows, grasp the loops; the stitching of these loops takes place as described in step 2.

- **Step 4:** When you finish the work, the loops of the last row must be chained off. To do this, crochet a warp stitch in the vertical wire of each machine.

How to Crochet in a Round

Crocheting in the round means you're going to stitch out your pattern. As a beginner, this is one of the most important things you could learn. Here's how:

1. First, you have to start chaining a ring. This will be your starting point. Make sure to chain 5, and then use a slip stitch for joining.

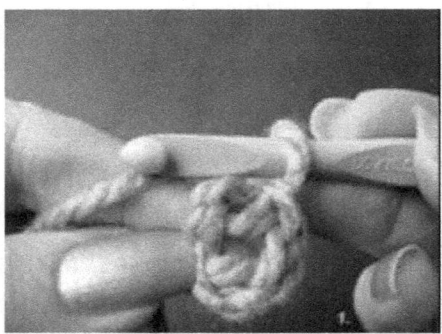

2. Next, start double crochet by making chain 2.

3. Now, check your pattern, and see how many double stitches you need for this round. For example, ten double crochets would make chain 2.

4. Then, join the stitches together by making a slip stitch. Do this on top of the chain at the row's beginning.

5. It's now time to make the next round of stitches. For this, you'd have to do chain 2.

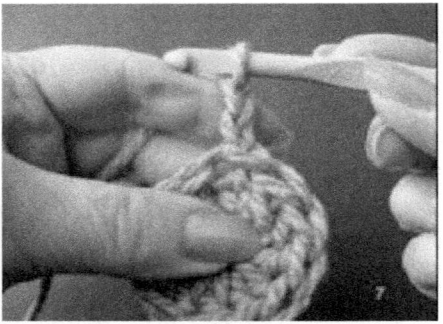

6. Now, you have to start working in the other direction. To do this, you have to turn your canvas. Just go on and continue working on the rest of the stitches.

7. Complete this round's needed number of stitches, and then join the round once more by making slip stitches.

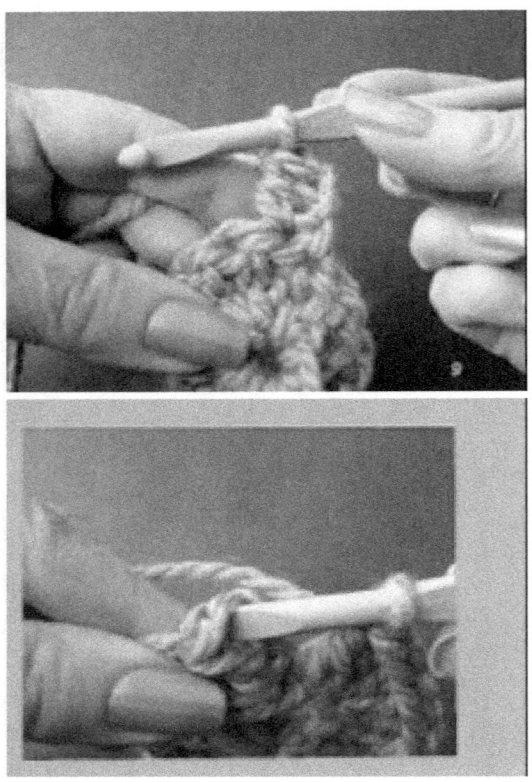

8. The arrow you see on the image below determines the position where you should make your slip stitches to keep the stitches joined.

When you do it right, you'll get a perfect round-shaped object, just like the one below.

Chapter 7: Holding the Yarn and the Hook

Just like we mentioned in holding the hook, there is also no right or wrong way to hold the yarn. The best way is the one that offers comfort and smooth crocheting. We usually hold the yarn in the non-dominant hand. This hand feeds the yarn to the hook in crocheting. The non-dominant hand also eases or increases the tension on the yarn to determine how loose or tight your patterns will be. When you are training to crochet, it is not easy to figure out how to hold the yarn. The good news is that it doesn't have to be easy. We have a basic way to hold the yarn that can be personalized to fit in your crocheting. Let us go through the steps on how to hold the yarn.

1. You should hold the hook in your dominant hand. Hold the hook with a knife grip or pencil grip, whichever gives you comfort. It helps you know the importance of yarn hold.

2. Use your other hand to hold the yarn. If the right hand is dominant, use the left one, and if your left hand is the dominant one, use the right one. Either of the holds will be the same, not considering the hand that will hold the yarn.

3. Spread your fingers and flatten your hand. By spreading your fingers, you will feed the yarn between them easily. Some people curve their fingers after the yarn is placed between the fingers as they feel comfortable that way.

4. You hold the beginning of the yarn with your thumb and index finger. In this next step, there are two ways of doing it. In the first method, some people hold the thread between their ring and pinkie from under the palm. In the second method, some people prefer holding the thread between their ring and middle finger. Either way is correct; what matters is your comfort.

5. Keep pulling the yarn to bring it diagonally over your hand. Some people pull at least 15cm from their index finger, while others prefer working with the yarn close to their hand.

6. To ease tension on your fingers, you should spread and close them to increase. Spreading and closing the fingers helps you to tighten and loosen your hold on the yarn. This movement of fingers is a cause of the type of pattern you are crocheting.

7. To have control over the yarn, you should hold it with your thumb and index finger. Press it between the two

fingers to increase or reduce the tension. Some people allow the yarn to dangle freely instead of pressing it between the thumb and index finger.

8. For security purposes, you should wrap the yarn on your pinkie finger. You should wrap it below your arm and hold it between your ring and pinkie finger. You should direct the yarn on top of your pinkie and then move it back between your ring and pinkie finger for a good hold on the yarn. By doing this, you will get more tension and also hold the yarn securely.

9. After the basic hold on the yarn, you should wrap it around your index finger. It should not be done tightly but should be comfy around your finger to avoid discomfort.

How Do You Find the Right Yarn Hold for Your Crochet?

We have read a lot about health issues caused by the way we hold our yarn. People have developed problems like carpal tunnel syndrome, tendonitis, or arthritis in the past caused by how they hold their hook with their dominant hand. However, we should also pay attention to the non-dominant hand that holds the yarn. As we mentioned earlier, it is important in regulating tension and providing a smooth crocheting motion. In crocheting, we should discover the method of holding the yarn that is suitable for each one of us.

Any method you choose to hold your yarn is correct only if it is effective in regulating the tension of the yarn and giving you comfort in the movement of your hands. Most people who crochet discover that their comfortable way of holding the yarn causes cramping or pain if they crochet for long periods. Some find that they need more physical effort when working with some stitch patterns. To some people, comfort in holding the yarn reduces their speed, and others form uneven spaced and sized stitches. Many people think that these problems are effects of the way they hold their hook, and some try adjusting it with no tangible results. Many others change their hook types with no visible effect. The truth, however, is these problems are a result of the way they hold and move their yarn.

Did that surprise you? Well, I didn't expect that either. The correct tension for good stitching requires a smooth movement of the yarn when the hook pulls it. If there is a big space between the yarn-guiding finger and the hook, the end stitches become loose on some parts. In such cases, the fingers hold tightly and might get some injuries, or you must keep adjusting the yarn through the fingers. It slows the work, injures the fingers, and causes uneven patterns on the fabric.

On the other hand, some people tighten the yarn around their palm or finger, causing difficulties in moving the yarn. The hook fights the resistance pulling the non-dominant hand with the force. It forces them to keep adjusting and wrapping the yarn again. The two methods above might result in a poor quality of the finished work, stress injuries, reduced speed in working, and messing the crochet rhythm.

Nonetheless, if we develop a system that can give two partial tension points, we would not need many muscles to regulate the movement of the yarn. If in crocheting, we can have a system that works like the sewing machine, we can reduce the different health issues caused by the way we hold our yarn. So, how can we develop such a system?

We can develop that through experiments and a lot of observation. We all have different shapes of the hands, such as narrow or wider palms, shorter or longer fingers. Some of us have more flexible hands than others, while others have more sweaty hands than others. All these unique features in our hands affect how we hold our yarn in one way or another. For instance, a person with arthritis will need a lot of effort to hold the yarn between the fingers, whereas a person whose fingers find it easy to hold may find it easy to hold the yarn between the fingers. Likewise, hands that sweat provides more friction than hands that do not sweat. Dry hands can be injured more easily than sweaty hands.

When you've held your yarn properly, and it is gently passing through your fingers, you apply tension in two places. By doing that, you can keep a good distance from the hook to work on the yarn. This distance should be short to be able to make even stitches. If you are using the index finger to guide the yarn, the distance between the hook and the guiding finger should not be more than an inch. In threadwork where the stitches should be tight, the distance should be less than that. The looseness of a stitch is a result of the amount of yarn in the mentioned distance.

So, you should start by making sure that your hands are straight and the palm should face you. If you have space between your fingers, then you should wrap the yarn around your pinky finger once instead of holding it with your fist. If there are no spaces between your fingers, then you should increase tension by entwining the yarn between your fingers. The next thing to observe should be your skin texture. Are your hands dry or moist? If they are moist, they will increase tension naturally and, therefore, few wrappings. If they are dry, you will wrap the pinky halfway as the yarn flows fast on dry hands, and it will be easy to keep.

How is the flexibility of your hands? Is it hard for you to bend your palm for the thumb and pinky to touch each other? If yes, you will have to guide the yarn using your middle finger. If it is easy for your thumb and pinky to touch, then you have a flexible hand; it will be easy to keep a good working distance. It is also good to change your style of holding the yarn to test its effectiveness. A change may be uncomfortable at first, but you should work through it to check if it will be painless. You never know; maybe a change is an answer to unswerving stitches with a painless procedure.

You are correctly holding the yarn while stitching, but are you looking out for the roll of yarn on the other end to keep it from tangling? Tangling of the yarn is an issue that disturbs even the most experienced people in this field. Working with several skeins of yarn can frustrate you as a yarn can tangle with itself or with the other colors. Tangling of the yarn waste a lot of time, and you might find yourself taking time to make some simple patterns than necessary. Let us look at some tips to keep your yarn from tangling as you are crocheting.

Roll Your Skeins into Balls of Yarn

Our skeins packaging is not an easy maneuver to work with. It is packed loosely and makes the skeins to tangle. Repackaging your skeins in a tight ball shape; this will ensure no tangling of the skein.

How Do You Pull Your Yarn?

I know we said earlier that there is no right way and wrong way to do it, but most crocheters agree that pulling your yarn from the center makes it tangle. The most advisable way to do it is to find the end of your yarn inside and pull from there. This way, the yarn slides without tangling out of the skein.

Container Use

In crocheting, you can't do away with creativity. Some crocheters have found it easy to crochet with their skeins inside a container. You should get a container and put your skein in it. Drill a hole where you will pull your yarn through. This method is effective as you keep your yarn away from the environment. It is advisable to get a clear container to keep you from checking the yarn size. If you are using more than one color, you can get more than one container.

Crochet Tension

What is crochet tension? In crocheting, tension is how tight the stitches are. It is also known as a gauge. Gauge is the number of stitches and rows per inch that are brought about by working with a specific yarn and hook size. How tight or lose your stitches are, is determined by how you hold your yarn, the type of hook you are using, and the thickness of your yarn. When you purchase yarn, the yarn label recommends the hook size to use and the gauge to achieve with that specific yarn. Tension affects the density, size, hang, and thickness of your crochet. It can also be affected by your posture or mood. It is important to get your crochet tension right always. So, how is crochet tension determined by how you hold your yarn?

Many beginners of crocheting hold the yarn too tightly. It makes the stitches hard, and crocheting the next row becomes even harder. It will also affect the end product of our crochet as it will be smaller than the size expected. Why is it so important to get the right tension on your yarn? Knowing the best tension to apply is important as it reflects on the results of your crochet. When crocheting, your yarn should flow smoothly through your fingers without inconsistencies. You should not strain it or let it hang loosely.

It is also important to know that we all crochet differently, and all crochets are not the same. Some are tighter than others. The most crucial thing in crocheting is your comfort in holding the yarn and hook. If the way you hold your yarn affects the gauge, we can change that with a few instructions. The best way to perfect your gauge is through practice, but there are different ways to reduce tension in your crochets.

Train Yourself to Pull the Yarn from the Center of the Skein

Every skein has an open end on the inside and outside. Many crocheters have confirmed that using the yarn from the outside causes the skein to keep bouncing everywhere, affecting your tension. When you pull your yarn from the center, it slides smoothly through your fingers. In some skeins, it is not easy to find the open end in the center; we should, therefore, be careful when doing it.

Wind the Skein into a Ball

It might take your time, but it reduces tension in your crochets. When you do this, you can get your yarn from any end you choose. You can also buy a ball winder, and it will help you combine two colors in one skein.

Yarn Bowl

Yarn bowls hold your yarn in place and keep it from tangling and falling into the arms of your children or pet, especially cats. A yarn bowl will save you a lot of trouble from the yarn bouncing all over the place, increasing tension to the yarn tangling.

Tension Regulator

It is easy to make and inexpensive. It is the best solution to regulating the tension. We wear a tension regulator on the base of the index finger, and you pass your yarn over its stitches. It regulates the tension on the yarn easily as it glides smoothly over the stitches.

Yarn Type

Tension can be a result of the type of yarn you are using. Some yarns like Lily Sugar 'N Cream are not beginner-friendly. I did not say it is not a great yarn, but inexperienced crocheters, they should work with stretchy yarns. Some yarns are not suitable for crocheters, still figuring out their tension. Hard and tough yarns also make it difficult for a beginner to count the stitches.

Hook Size

To know whether to use a large or small hook size, you should look at your first row and foundation chain. If both of them are loose, you should change to a smaller hook, and if they are tight, then a bigger one would be good to go. You should play up and down your hook size to get the correct tension.

Are You a Tight or Loose Crocheter?

As I mentioned earlier, we all crochet differently, and it is acceptable. If you are a loose crocheter, you should change your hook to a smaller one than recommended, and if you are a tight crocheter, you should get a larger hook.

How to Hold the Hook When Crocheting

The hook must be held properly while doing crochet work. This will reduce the incidence of pain in your wrist and will even make your work go on smoothly. There are two major methods mentioned in crochet literature; they are the pencil hold and the knife hold.

- **The pencil hold:** One way of gripping your hook is by holding it with your thumb, index, and middle finger. You can just imitate the way you'll hold your writing pencil.

- **The knife hold:** You can also hold it like your knife, with your palm on the handle, your three fingers wrapped around it, and your index finger pointing towards the head of the hook.

Which of the two methods mentioned above is better?

In the real sense, we all have different ways of handling stuff. We all hold our writing pencils differently, and it is part of what accounts for the differences in handwriting. Two different people might also have different ways of holding the knife. So, I will say, find the style that suits you and crochet away!

Right and Wrong Sides of a Crochet Piece

In the art of crochet, working on the wrong side might lead the crocheter into making errors and, therefore, result in frogging. Working on the wrong side can also give a crochet result that is entirely different from what the crocheter had in mind (or in the picture).

How do you avoid working on the wrong side of a crochet piece?

You can avoid this by not doing any crochet on the tail of the yarn. The tail of the yarn is the length of the yarn between your piece and the ball or skein of yarn. For the piece to be on the right side, the tail should be at the bottom right corner.

How to Differentiate the Front and Back of a Chain Stitch?

While some authorities will tell you to work from back to the front, others might instruct you to do the reverse. Also, while some will ask you to make the front loop only (flo), the back loop only (blo) might turn out to be the focus of some other instructional guides. Not following these instructions might lead you to end up with a design that is different from what you had in mind before you started. The front of a loop looks like Vs sitting on top of one another while the back looks like humps.

Frogging (Undoing Crochet)

Frogging in crocheting terms simply means to correct an error. Stitches that have been crocheted in error can be ripped out and remade. You just have to be patient and gentle with the fabric when doing so. Frogging can both be easy and painful at the same time.

You just have to pull out your hook and rip it off till you get to the point where the error was made and just continue again. You can roll the frogged yarn into a ball or around the material to prevent it from tangling. What's most painful? You have no choice but to do it again as soon as frogging occurs! It is advisable to mark the point where you stop frogging with a stitch marker to avoid ripping beyond the necessary point.

When you are frogging, you should not be very fast with it. Instead, to make your frogging smooth, you need to be slow-paced enough to detach the stitches from the base of the stitch and not pulling upwards.

You may have knots in your work (points where you had to join a piece of yarn to the other), and when you get to points like this, you should be careful to untie the knot first. If it is tightly tied and can't be untied, cut it off.

Crotchet can also be frogged entirely to reclaim it. You can decide to use the yarn to make something else, and so frogging becomes necessary.

Chapter 8: How to Crochet for Left-Handers

For the left-handed crafters out there, you are well aware of how confusing it can be to follow right-handed methods and adjust them to suit your needs. Crochet patterns and instructions are made for right-handers unless otherwise mentioned.

There are so few left-handed crafters, and being a minority, there are not many sources available to learn from. This is because only a small percentage of people are left-handed, and most of them are men. So, when it comes to doing crafts, particularly crafts for women, instructions for left-handers are not a priority.

Most left-handed women use right-handed instructional tools and prefer to use those. They end up learning how to crochet with their right hand. This may be alright for some, whereas others don't have as much coordination in their right hand to create a smooth rhythm. It is also possible to follow right-handed instructions and adjust them accordingly so that you can use your left hand to crochet. This can work, but it is confusing at times, and one needs to concentrate carefully.

So, if you are a lefty and you intend to take up crochet as a hobby, this guide should be very useful, and hopefully, it will make the process a lot easier for you.

Let's Get Started

The most important thing is to get a firm and comfortable grip on your crochet hook, as this will allow you to proceed to the next step. So, once you have a grip on it with your left hand, you'll need to use your right hand for holding the yarn. This is simply the opposite of what right-handers do.

You choose, as right-handers do, to hold your crochet hook using your thumb and your index finger to keep it in place, or you can simply grip it as you would a knife. Both ways are easy to get used to, so just decide which one you prefer using and learn to crochet that way.

There are, of course, several ways that you can hold your yarn as you work your stitches, and that is up to you. One of the most commonly used methods is to loop the yarn using your right index finger. Keep the loose end up and then allow the thread that is attached to the yarn to lie on your palm in a cross manner. Once you have done this, you can use the free end of the yarn to create a slip knot to start the crochet process.

Once you have done that, using your right hand then hold the slip knot you have made between your fingers' middle and thumb. This is the most comfortable position for this. Your yarn will be between your index finger and your thumb, so you'll be able to control your tension nicely using your index finger. Controlling your tension will help you to create consistent, even stitches. It is best to master this from the beginning, as it will make a huge difference to the quality of your work later on.

What Is the Difference Between Right and Left-Handed Crafters?

Although it is confusing to change hands when crocheting, the main differences between right-handed and left-handed techniques are as follows:

- You either grip your crochet hook in your right or left hand.
- You'll hold the yarn in your free hand.
- The direction you work in changes as a left-hander, as you'll work your stitches from left to right, whereas a right-hander will do the opposite.
- To work the stitches in rounds, left-handers will work in a counter-clockwise direction to the right. Right-handers will do the opposite and work their stitches in a clockwise direction to the left.
- Crochet rounds worked by left-handers have a different appearance compared to those made by right-handers. Although some right-handed crocheters think that left-handers' rounds look odd, others actually prefer them.
- Rows worked by left-handers look the same as those done by right-handers, except that the yarn has been fastened off on the other end, so that is the only difference.

- Once you start, you'll have a piece of yarn that hangs down; this is your yarn tail. Always leave the tail hanging and never crochet over it. If a pattern has a right side and a wrong side of the work, your tail can be used to give you a hint. When the tail is hanging on the bottom right-hand corner, then that makes it the right side to work on.
- Each time that you do the yarning over, you will pick up the yarn in a clockwise direction. This is a good point to remember at all times.

Working from Graphs

As a left-handed crafter, you'll find that most of the difficulties will lie in the interpretation of the patterns and graphs that you might use. Written patterns will be a challenge, whereas symbols are easier to use.

As an absolute beginner, you may not use graphs to start with. However, you are bound to come across them later on and use them. There are two different ones which you will use. The first is a graph used for color changes in your rows. These graphs make use of colored squares to represent the stitches. Hence, a red square indicates a red stitch in that row.

The second type of graph that you'll need to read is the graph used for the filet crochet technique. These are more complex and can be intimidating at first. The graph consists of blocks, which are filled in, and they represent three double crochet stitches, which are worked into three separate stitches in the row above.

There are also open squares on the graph, and these are the mesh, consisting of double crochet and also chain stitches.

These graphs are marked with numbers representing the rows and stitches and are made for right-handed workers. Hence, as a left-hander, you'll need to alter the graph accordingly. If you are not confident in doing so, you will still be able to use the graph as it is. However, the design will be reversed and won't be exactly the same. This is not such a problem when it comes to basic designs and pictures but bear in mind that if there are any words on the graphs, they will appear as mirror images in the final product.

Here are some left-hander tips for reading graphs:

Left-handers should read the first row of the graph in the opposite direction, from left to right. Remember that right-hander will read it from right to left.

The stitches in filet graphs are normally different, but the graphs read the same. For example, the first row that falls on your right side is normally read from the left side onto the right; this is the front side of the work done.

The first row of the right side gives you a basis of your work (front of work) will be read from left to right, which means the work is okay, while the wrong side (back of work) will be read from right to left.

Generally, the common patterns can be used by everyone, whether right or left-handed. Most of them will need to be changed slightly and also reversed. You'll learn how to do this by trial and error.

A basic adjustment that you might need to make is as follows: join the yarn in the top left-hand corner of your piece. You'll need to do the opposite, of course, and join the yarn you are using to the upper right hand, and to be specific, in the corner. Most times, you will just need to reverse instructions such as these.

There is no need to avoid using a pattern because it is not made specifically for left-handers. The more you practice, the easier it becomes until eventually adjusting your patterns will become a habit.

Left-Handed Crocheting

Being left-handed needn't stop you from learning to crochet. It may seem challenging at first; after all, most patterns are aimed at right-handed users and attempting to manage these will have you working backward. Below are a few ways to get around this:

1. Reverse the pattern so that you're holding the crochet hook in your right hand. This means that the 'wrong side' of the pattern is actually 'the right side.'

2. Practice holding the hook until you're comfortable. A lot of left-handed crocheters have created their own variation on the 'pencil' or 'knife' hold in a way that suits them.

3. Learn by sitting across from someone right-handed, mirroring their movements!

Creating Your Own Pattern

You may get to a stage where you have been crocheting for a while, and you'd like to try your hand at creating your own pattern.

To do this, there are a few things you should keep in mind:

- Master all the basic crochet stitches before you start, so you know the appearance and usage of each one.
- Follow a variety of patterns, noticing the mechanics of how they put a project together.
- Learn to count stitches and rows, so you'll be able to work them into your own.
- Experiment as much as you can with materials, tools, and ideas.
- Get decorative with your creations. Practice with shapes and styles.
- Try to modify an existing pattern for practice.
- Learn how a gauge works—it's a great way to calculate stitches effectively.

- Sketch what you'd like to create to assist you in the shapes you'll need.
- Start simple and small, building complexity as you get used to it.
- Write everything down as you go, and maybe allow other crocheters to practice your pattern to get a better idea of how it'll work.

Chapter 9: Tips and Tricks to Crocheting

Every crocheter requires tips and tricks to become a pro. These tips and tricks make things easier when you begin crocheting.

Crocheting Using Thread

When it comes to crocheting thread, remember that smaller is bigger. Threads are labeled according to their thickness. The thicker the thread, the smaller is the number. It is counterintuitive, but the more you crochet, the more you will get used to it.

1. As a beginner, you can always start with a crochet thread three, then move up to a five and ten. Size twenty or thirty threads can be used once you have built up your skills.
2. As with the crochet threads, follow the same approach with steel crochet hooks. The smaller the size, the bigger the crochet hook. You can also look at the mm size that is usually printed on the hook itself. For example, a hook sized nine is 1.25 mm while the hook sized ten is 1.15 mm.
3. As a beginner, you should start with a hook size that the pattern calls for. Once you have honed your skills a little more, you can adjust your hooks based on your comfort level and gauge.

4. For beginners, it is always good to use steel crochet hooks. These hooks are much easier to use when it comes to working with thread.

5. People often find crocheting using thread more difficult compared to using yarn, and it is only because of the thinner hooks involved. When you are working with the thread, all you need to do is choose a hook that has a bigger handle—that's all!

6. When purchasing thread, always buy a crochet thread and steer clear from embroidery or sewing thread. Although you can crochet with almost anything that resembles yarn or thread, you can make your life easier by sticking to the kind of thread that is meant for crocheting.

7. When you work with yarn overs, make sure to work closely with the crochet hook head. You always want to ensure that the work on the hook is done above the section of the hook, where it starts to get wider. Otherwise, your loops will be extremely loose.

8. Another tip would be to thread around your non-crocheting hand, so it is easier to control your tension. This is extremely helpful when thread crocheting.

Crocheting Hacks with Yarn

1. To prevent the balls of yarn from falling and rolling away while you are crocheting, put them in a hand wipe container. Just make sure to wash and clean it first. The

yarn can be pulled through the hole of the hand wipe container.

2. Use bobby pins or safety pins, or even a paper clip to mark your rows, or stitch a colored yarn or thread into the valley of the first stitch. Bobby pins and paper clips can be pulled out later once you are done.

3. Use pencil boxes or jewelry boxes, or even a toothbrush holder to store your hooks. Food and snack containers can also do the trick.

4. Use Excel sheets to map out your patterns. This is a great way to keep track of where you left off when your crocheting gets interrupted. You can also make the pattern larger to decrease eye strain.

5. To figure out the amount of yarn or thread needed for a certain project, calculate the number of rows you can get out of one skein/ball, and determine how many rows your project requires. Then, divide the number of rows the project requires by the number of rows your ball gives you. You will be able to calculate how much yarn is needed this way.

6. If you are worried about purchasing too much colored yarn that you won't be using in the future, just buy white washable yarn and dye it according to the pattern's colors.

7. To keep your project in place, use yarn needles instead of hooks to weave the ends back through. This holds the

project better and eliminates the chances of the yarn traveling.

8. Dip the end of the yarn in clear nail polish to make it go through the eye of a needle. When you dip it, twist the yarn tight while it dries.

9. Instead of ironing your projects, which is not always ideal, mix water and starch in equal parts and spray liberally on your project; leave to dry on a flat surface.

10. To store patterns in a three-ring notebook, use sheet protectors.

11. Keeping an index card with the lists of hooks and yarns you have is a great way to keep inventory. This ensures that the next time you are short of crochet supplies, you already know what you need.

12. Yarns and other unfinished projects can be kept in zipper bags.

13. It is always a good idea to keep foldable sewing scissors so that they don't snag in your crocheting bag.

14. When in doubt, sew more tightly with string than you would with yarn. Try not to stitch so firmly that you hurt your hands. Knit somewhat more firmly than normal (except if you're now a skilled crocheter, at that point, simply do what you generally do!).

15. Pay attention to the steps you're about to follow before you figure with thread crochet. Jumping from an acceptable hook size, worked with a cumbersome yarn all

the way down to thread crochet, can make your thread paintings appear unbearably tiny. Steadily work your way down to the smaller sizes.

16. Always do your crochet work in a good light so that you don't strain your eyes. This also makes crocheting easier. This is the same reason why, as beginners, you need to work with a lighter colored thread as it makes it easier for you to find those little stitches.

17. Crocheting is fun! Sure, it does have its own challenges, but that's only something you'll need to overcome at the beginning. Learning takes time, so be patient with yourself and enjoy each project you work on.

18. Always choose beginner patterns when you're starting. This will make it easier for you to learn how to combine stitches and learn the ropes of crocheting.

19. Working with a simple crochet swatch that uses basic stitches is always ideal, just to get the best results, minus the pressure of going through with a pattern.

Chapter 10: Easy and Fun Crochet Pattern for Beginners

Having looked at the techniques of making the stitch, then comes the part where you want to begin with some natural patterns before you graduate into the more complicated stitches.

Through the proper use of the hook and yarn, you should be able to master crochet in a short time with repeated practice, and to begin your practice, we have identified some simple patterns that you could use to start with your crochet.

Remember, to gain fast and become almost like a pro, so practice is critical. Begin with these natural patterns, master them, and challenge yourself to graduate to more intricate models.

The first step that many experts in crochet recommend before you take to your first attempt is to read the title of the crochet. This is that you understand what the patterns will be for—blanket, scarf, sweater, etc. So, before setting down, start by reading the title.

Crochet Purse Bag

Easy, simple, and eye-catching—talk about aesthetical and functional. Have fun making this in rainbow shades, gradient shades, or alternate between your favorite colors.

1st Round

1. Make a Magic Ring.

2. Make 3 Chains and 12 DCs into the Magic Ring.

3. Slip stitch into the 1st stitch you started and fasten off. You should have 13 stitches in total.

2nd Round

Change yarn color.

1. Make a DC into one of the stitches from the early row. Pass in a 2nd DC into the same stitch.

2. Finish this round by making 2 DCs in each stitch from the previous round.

3. Slip stitch into the 1st stitch you found and fasten off. You should have 26 DCs in total.

3rd Round

Change yarn color.

1. Start with 1 DC into any stitch from the previous round.

2. In the next stitch, make 2 DCs into the same stitch, and make 1 DC in the next stitch.

3. Repeat step 2 until you finish this round, alternating between 2 DCs and 1 DC.

4. Slip stitch into your 1st stitch and fasten off. You should have 39 DCs.

4th Round

Change yarn color.

1. Make two DCs in two separate stitches.

2. Make 2 DCs into one stitch.

3. Repeat steps 1 and 2 until you finish this round, alternating between 2 DCs in two separate stitches and one 2 DCs in the same stitch.

4. Slip stitch into the 1st stitch you planned and fasten off. You should have 52 DCs.

5th Round

Change yarn color.

1. In this round, make 3 DCs in three separate stitches and sewing in 2 DCs into the 4th stitch.

2. Keep alternating between 3 DCs in three separate stitches and fastening in 2 DCs into the 4th stitch

3. Slipstitch into the first stitch you made and fasten off. You should have 65 DCs.

6th Round

Change yarn color.

1. In this round, make 4 DCs in three separate stitches, and stitch in 2 DCs into the 5th stitch.

2. Keep alternating between 4 DCs in three separate stitches and fastening in 2 DCs into the 5th stitch.

3. Slipstitch into the first stitch you made and fasten off. You should have 78 DCs.

7th Round

Change yarn color.

1. In this round, make 5 DCs in three separate stitches and sewing in 2 DCs into the 6th stitch.

2. Keep alternating between 5 DCs in three separate stitches and fastening in 2 DCs into the 6th stitch

3. Slipstitch into the first stitch you made and fasten off. You should have 91 DCs.

How to Assemble

1. With a needle and thread, sew in a zipper on half of the circle.

2. Fold over, and sew in the other half onto the other side of the zipper.

3. Embellish with beads and sequins or leave it as is.

Crochet Flowers

These flowers are crocheted with wool for a crochet hook of strength 4 in rounds, and each of them is closed with a Kettmasche.

- Close the chain of 6 meshes with a chain stitch to the ring.
- 1st round: 12 fixed sts.
- 2nd round: in every M. 2 tr. (Replace the first trump with 3 ch.)
- 3rd round: Instead of the first tr. 3 ch., then into the first st. 1 tr., in the next M. Crochet 1 tr. and 1 half tr.

* At the following 4 m. in each puncture site 1 solid st., 1 half st. and 1 st., then 2 st., in the 4. Crochet 1 tr. and 1 half tr. *

Repeat 4 times and replace the 6th sheet with 1 solid M., 1 complete half tr. and 1 tr. Cut the thread and pull it through. You can combine several individual motifs into one flower, or you can stitch together two individual motifs in different colors. Thus, simple blankets and crocheted with raffia, even carpets.

Maybelle Flower Coasters

Make these vintage crochet flower motifs into gorgeous coasters. Gradient, variegated, solid, or change colors for every row to make these coasters more personalized.

Note: For this pattern, I recommend you use a chunky cotton yarn along with an appropriately sized hook.

1st Round

1. Chain 10 and slip stitch into your 1st stitch to form a circle.

2. Chain 3, this will count as your 1st DC for this round.

3. Make 23 more DCs

4. Then slip stitch into your 1st stitch.

2nd Round

1. Chain 5 then SC into the 3rd stitch from the base of your chain.

2. Repeat step 1 until you finish this row.

3. Slip stitch into the 1st chain you made. You should have 8 half circles in total.

3rd Round

1. Slip stitch into the chain space.

2. In the same chain space, chain 3 (this will be your 1st DC) make 1 more DC, chain 2, 2 more DCs, and 1 chain.

3. Repeat step 2 into all the chain spaces. Changing the 1st chain 3 into 1 DC.

4. Slip stitch into the 1st stitch you made.

4th Round

1. Stitch your way into the 1st chain space of 2.

2. In the same chain space, chain 3 and make 6 DCs, and 1 SC into the Chain of 1 from the previous round.

3. Make 7 DCs into the chain space of 2, and then 1 SC into the next chain of 1 from the previous round.

4. Repeat step 4 until you've made fan stitches of 7 DCs into each chain space of 2.

5. Slip stitch into your 1st stitch, fasten off, and tuck in ends.

Yarn Basket

Have you ever worked with T-Shirt yarn before? This will be a great pattern to start with! Even though this pattern works with any kind of yarn, I suggest you use a T-Shirt yarn.

Note: This is well with any kind of yarn; just make sure you use the appropriate hook according to the yarn's thickness. It is important to check tension and maintain even stitches.

1st Round

1. Start with making 3 chains and slip stitching into the 1st stitch to make a ring.

2. Make 7 SCs into the ring.

2nd Round

1. SC 2 in each stitch. You should have 14 SCs when you finish this round.

3rd Round

1. Alternate making 1 SC in one stitch, and then 2 SCs in one stitch. You should have 21 SCs when you finish this round.

4th Round

1. Alternate making 2 SCs in the next two stitches, 2 SCs in one stitch. You should have 28 SCs when you finish this round.

5th Round

1. Alternate making 3 SCs in the next three stitches, 2 SCs in one stitch. You should have 35 SCs when you finish this round.

6th Round

1. Alternate making 4 SCs in the next four stitches, 2 SCs in one stitch. You should have 42 SCs when you finish this round.

7th Round

1. Alternate making 5 SCs in the next five stitches, 2 SCs in one stitch. You should have 49 SCs when you finish this round.

8th Round

1. Make SCs in the back loops of each stitch. You should have 49 SCs when you finish this round.

9th to 16th Round

1. Make SCs around, maintaining 49 stitches for each round.

17th Round

1. Make 22 SCs, then chain 9 to make a handle, skip 3 stitches, SC in the next 21 stitches.

2. Chain 9 and skip 3 stitches again to make the second handle.

18th Round

1. Continue making SCs around the rim.

2. When you reach the handles, SC over the stitches, making as many as needed to cover the stitches from the previous round.

3. Slip stitch, fasten off and tuck in the ends.

Simple Dishcloth

What you need:

- 1 skein cotton yarn
- I snare

Guidelines:

Chain 25

Column 1: Into the third chain from your snare, half twofold sew until the finish of the establishment chain—you should now have 22 lines over. Chain 2 and turn.

Line 2: Half twofold sew multiple times, chain 2 at that point turn. Proceed until you have 16 columns—don't attach off.

1. Include a solitary stitch column all-round the 4 sides of your material. Start by placing one single knit in the join you are taking a shot at this point. Pivot the fabric so as to stitch down the left side.
2. A single stitch in each space down the side—it shouldn't be precise, simply guarantee it is even as you go down; in any case, your fabric will pack.

Ear Warmer

What you need:

- 5.00 mm snare
- Embroidered artwork needle
- Scissors
- Worsted weight yarn

Directions:

Chain 56

Line 1: Slip joint into the primary chain.

Column 2: Start working in adjusts; chain 1 and a half twofold sew around, then join to the primary half twofold sew.

1. Rehash line 2 until you have 8 columns—you can include more whenever wanted.
2. Attach off and leave a long tail.
3. To secure the ear hotter, string the tail into your yarn needle. Gather the seamed segment of your headband and crease it into half, guaranteeing that the overlay is confronting you.
4. Bring both of the sides to the head of your crease and secure it set up.
5. Run the needle through all the segments of the material you have accumulated.
6. Fold your yarn over the underside of your snap, then through the areas again. Do this multiple times, so you secure the snap, attach the end and weave in the tail.

Colorful Pimples

It looks happy when you work the pimples in different colors. In addition, you can meaningfully use small yarn remnants in this way.

To crochet a colored nub, work the last solid stitch in front of the nub in the base color until there are still two loops on the needle to finish the stitch with the yarn for the nub. Then crochet the nub as described in the new color. Use the chain stitch to secure the knob; work again in the basic color, with which you then continue crocheting until the next knob.

Flat Nubs

Flat knobs are made of half-sticks and are slightly less plastic than knobs or the popcorn stitches described below. They are often used to crochet baby clothes and cuddly blankets. They are crocheted according to the same principle as the pimples. It is important that you do not work too hard. The following example illustrates how to crochet a flat knot of three half rods in one go through all the loops on the needle. It is advisable to secure the knit stitch with a chain stitch (take the thread and pull it once again through the stitch on the needle) so that the stitches remain firmly together at the top, and the knobby effect maintains the desired plasticity.

1. First, thread the thread around the needle, and then insert it into the loop into which the flat knot should be placed. Get the thread.

2. Repeat this step twice so that there are finally seven loops on the crochet hook. Then you pick the thread and pull it in one go through all the loops.

3. Finally, secure the flat knot with a warp stitch by retrieving the thread and pulling it through the loop on the crochet hook.

Filet or Net Pattern

For this effective but, in principle, quite simple pattern, you crochet a grid from bars and air meshes. You can combine filled and empty boxes in such a way that geometric or floral motifs are created. A simple net pattern without "fillings" can be crocheted very fast. For example, it is good for light scarves and bandages, and if you can handle it with sturdy material works, you would have crocheted, in no time, a shopping net. If you work alternately filled and empty boxes, you can pull a cord through the stitches to close about a bag.

1. Crochet a chain of meshes first. The number of stitches for your basic chain must be divisible by two. In addition, crochet six more pieces of air.

2. Now, for the first box, insert into the sixth stitch of the chain of stitches as seen from the needle and work a chopstick.

3. Crochet an airlock again. For the subsequent chopsticks, pass over a stitch in the sling chain. Then, crochet one more air mesh and the next chopstick into

the next, but one mesh of the basic chain work. So, continue until the end of the series.

4. Start the next row with three first-streaks and one streak with the next-stick link.

5. Now, work a chopstick into the scraping member of the penultimate stick of the previous row, crochet a loop of air, pass one stitch of the previous row, and work another stick into the corresponding chopsticks of the previous row. The last stitch of the row works in the third link of the chain of meshes counted from below.

6. To crochet a filled box, do not join the sticks with an airlock, but crochet between the base sticks other sticks around the air mesh of the previous row. To do this, just stick in the empty box to get the thread.

7. If the box of the previous row is also filled, work the "stuffing stick" into the scraping member of the pre-row filler.

Grid Pattern

A likewise light and transparent pattern is the grid pattern, which is crocheted from air mesh and solid or warp stitches.

Experimental minds vary the length of the air chains to work an uneven lattice structure.

Normally, the arcs are one-third longer than the basic piece of the previous series. The arcs in the following instructions are five air mesh long, the base three chains.

1. Work an air chain. The number of stitches should be divisible by four. For this crochet, add two air meshes.

2. Now, anchor the first bow by crocheting it into the sixth stitch of the base with a slit stitch or a sturdy stitch. Then crochet five loops of air, pass three meshes in the basic loop and anchor the bow in the fourth loop of the air.

3. The last bow of the row is attached in the last loop of the base chain.

4. Now, crochet five air stitches and then a single crochet stitch into the bow, then another five stitches, and then a single crochet stitch into the next bow. The last bow is anchored in the third spiral of the first row.

5. Start the next series again with five air stitches, fasten them with a sturdy stitch in the first loop of air mesh, and work in the grid pattern to the end of the row. The last tight stitch back into the third spiral air mesh of

the front row work. Continue working until the desired height is reached.

DIY Scarves

Scarves are often rather straight forward when it comes to crochets, and you will find yourself making them rather quickly with the movements that you have learned so that you do it efficiently and within a short time.

When you have finished creating the foundation chain, you will then use the turning chain to create a long thin rectangle that you can keep knitting depending on how long and thus, how thick you want the scarf to be. As a beginner, this is a task that could take you a couple of hours a day, but you will be much satisfied with the outcome once you make it past the first couple of stitches.

Granny Square

This is a prevalent crochet pattern, and therefore, you will find great value in learning how to go through it.

You will begin by creating the slip knot and then creating three chains. Then you start using the double crochet so that you end up with double stitches. Once you do this, loop the two double stitches through the third chain.

After this, create another three of such dc clusters, but now you will move the dc into the foundation of the first round.

When you finish with this, repeat the first two steps. Then, repeat this process, beginning with a new foundation chain from the end of one dc stitch as you create the stitching until you get to the size of the granny square that you want.

You will then use the granny square on whatever you may want, from small table mats to covers for items in the house such as sound systems and TV sets. Depending on how you have woven it, you can also use it as a cover for pillows or small furniture like stools.

You can make several squares and then join them, make one huge Granny square and add a border, or mix squares and rows of Granny stitches for a pretty effect. In this chapter, we'll learn how to crochet a Granny square and a few easy and pretty ways to join your squares.

Example of a big Granny Square throw

If you want a perfectly square Granny square, then simply turn the square each time you begin a new round. This will prevent the classic lean found in the center of larger squares.

To begin chain 4 and join with a slip stitch in the first chain to form a ring. The stitches are now worked into the ring, not into the chain stitches. Chain 3 and work 2 double crochet. Chain 3 and work 3 double crochet three more times until you have four sets of chain 3 and 3 chain stitches. Join with a slip stitch into the 3rd chain of the beginning chain 3. This is Round 1.

Begin Round 2 by either slip stitching to the first chain 3 space or joining a new color into a chain 3 space. Chain 3 and work 2 double crochet, chain 3, 3 double crochet into the first chain 3 space. Chain 1 in the next chain 3 space work 3 double crochet, chain 3, 3 double crochet, chain 1. Repeat this around the square and join with a slip stitch into the 3rd chain of the starting chain. This is Round 2.

Join new color in any chain 3 corner space.

Round 2 using the same color as Round 1.

Begin Round 3 by either slip stitching to the next chain 3 space or joining a new color in any chain 3 corner space. Into the first corner space, work chain 3, 2 double crochet, chain 3, 3 double crochet, chain 1. In the next chain 1 space, work 3 double crochet and a chain 1. Into each corner space (chain 3 spaces) work 3 double crochet, chain 3, 3 double crochet, chain 1. Into each chain 1 space work 3 double crochet, chain 1. When you reach the beginning chain 3, slip stitch into the 3rd chain to finish this round.

To add rounds to the square, either slip stitch to the next chain 1 or chain 3 space or join new color in any chain 3 corner space. Into each corner, work 3 double crochet, chain 3, 3 double crochet, chain 1 (the very first set of 3 double crochet will be chain 3 and 2 double crochet). Into each chain 1 space work 3 double crochet, chain 1. Add as many rows as you like to your square to make it as large as you want.

Joining Methods

Once you get all of your squares crocheted, you will need to join them. There are many methods you can use to join squares. In this section, we'll go over three of the most popular and easy methods you can use to join your squares; whip stitch, slip stitch, and single crochet.

Whip stitch join method

To use the whip stitch to join the squares, thread a tapestry or blunt end needle with yarn. Give yourself plenty of yarn to work with when you thread your needle. Hold two squares with right sides together and line up the edge stitches. Insert the needle under the outer loops only of the edges stitches and sew the squares together. This method gives you a nice lacy look between the squares and is very easy.

- Catch only the outer loops in the whip stitches
- Completed whip stitch join

Slip stitch join method

The second method is the slip stitch join. Hold two squares with the right sides together and line up the stitches. Join the yarn in a corner space and then slip stitch the edge stitches of both squares together. You can either catch both loops of the edge stitches in the slip stitches or just catch the outer loops for a different look. When you come to a corner where you are joining the next set of squares, slip stitch into the corner of the first set, chain 1, and then slip stitch into the corner of the next set. When joining four squares, slip stitch around the chain 1 space of the two sets to make a nice neat corner join.

Single Crochet Join Method

The single crochet join creates a decorative raised edging around the squares. I use this method a lot because I like the look of the join and how it frames each square. Hold two squares together with the wrong sides together and match up the stitches. Join the yarn in the corner space and chain 1. Work a single crochet into the corner space, and then single crochet the squares together. When you come to the other corner, work a single crochet into the corner space, chain 1, and single crochet into the corner space of the next two squares.

When you are joining strips of squares and come to the corner single crochet into the corner space, and single crochet around the chain 1 space between the sets of squares, and then single crochet into the next corner space, this creates a nice neat corner and retains the ridged look of the join.

In the following example, the vertical join is single crochet, and the horizontal join is a slip stitch, so you can see the difference in the stitches.

Here are two schemes that will help you:

Crochet Socks

Crochet socks are other designs that you will find it easier to do when you are a beginner.

According to Clara Parkes, the best yarns for socks are those that are elastic, meaning that they will need to stretch when you dip your foot into it, then wrap around the foot comfortably and warmly once you have worn it.

You will use your basic crochet techniques when you do this, while you will need additional experience to make more complex socks like ankle-high socks and those with frilled edges or fancy patterns.

However, if you want simple, ankle-length socks, here you will need to alternate between single crochet and double crochet. You will alternate between these two, lapping them over each other as you move through the foundations' chains, leaving the fabric closely knit. This is what we call the seed stitch crochet.

So, you are with your foundation chain, then flip it over and begin to work on the turning chain, and make the first stitch, which will work as your first double crochet in the first row. Then, start to alternate between the dc and sc. Once you make your first dc, make the sc after that, then the dc, sc as you progress. Then make these stitches across the rows. When you start with a dc, you will then end the row with sc.

Once you finish, turn it over and begin working on the turning chain. But since you will have flipped over the wool, you will be working in reverse, your dc going above sc and your sc going above dc.

To continue creating the rows that you need, repeat the process from the moment when you made your first dc. You will repeat this process depending on how long you want the socks to be, though as a beginner, you should probably make it as short as possible as you work on your hand movements and ironing out the problems that may arise when you make a mistake.

Crochet Seat Covers

You will find these in many homes and cars, providing the room with an antique, authentic, and comforting feel. And the thing about these is that the patterns are relatively easy to follow, with the size and design also mainly depending on how you want it. But you will want to keep it straight if you're going to create extensive material.

Once you have done your slip knot and created your foundation chain, make four stitches and two rows. Then, in the first round, create eight single crochet stitches and make two sc stitches in each stitch.

As with the socks, you will alternate between dc and sc. Once you create the two first rows, create another chain. Then, on the first row, the fourth chain from the hook make dc through until the end of the row. Then, on the second chain, on the second row, make double crochet until the end. Repeat this on the third row, third chain. Once you have finished these, then close the terms. At this point, you will have a square granny design, and you will then work from here through with additional rows and chains depending on how long you want it to be and how much you want it to cover the seat.

However, if you want to add on color and make it larger, create additional rows and chains using wool from the color that you want to infuse to the cover.

Square Blanket

This is one other straightforward pattern that you can learn. This one will also turn out great with just one color, though you will then have to put a lot of time into it so that you can achieve the thickness and size that you want.

Using the basis of the granny square, make your foundation chain, and create three more. Begin to make double crochets, then loop them to create double stitches. After this, connect these two double stitches through the third chain. Then, create another three dc but with the dc going into the foundation of the first round.

Go through this step until you get to the size that you desire. For extra thickness, you could use the technique of socks and use alternating dc and sc to create additional loops and knots to the width that you desire.

Alternatively, you can still use this basis to create a table cover, but then you will not need to make it substantial and thick as you would have with a blanket.

Crochet Sweater for Beginners

The basis of making the sweater is starting from how you would make the granny square. Make two of such rectangles, with the size depending on who you are making for. Use dc for making the rectangle that you will make the front so that it is one solid piece with minimal gaps. You could also use this for the back or use sc to leave a see-through back for extra aesthetics.

So, create nine chains with two rows. Here, make an "sc" through the second chain from the hook. Make a total of 8 sc. In the second row, stitch across the first chain, back loops only (blo). Then repeat this with the second row to row 65 or above, depending on the size to fit on waist, chest, and hips. Note that you will need the rows to be odd numbers.

Then move to the first row, and in the first chain, turn it and make sc across the band, with one running across each row, down to the number of rows that you have for the sweater and the region it fits. In the second row, loop through the third chain, turn and make double crochet across all rows. In the third row, repeat the second process. Through the fourth row to the seventh, make the stitches on the chain lose.

Then in the 8th row, go through the third chain, turn it and make a double crochet in each dc and chain space so that you create a close-knit loop through each row until the end. In the 9th row, the third chain makes dc across all rows until the end. Use this technique for the back rectangle, but then you will use sc and dc alternately depending on if you want the gaps or not.

Crochet with Plastic Rings

Pure fun brings crocheting with plastic rings. A brisk job that brings results quickly. However, you should not crochet the rings individually but create coherent chains.

Making a Crochet Ring

To start, put the normal crochet start loop on the plastic ring. The loop for the first solid ash and all subsequent hands is always pulled through the ring. Then, as usual, the two loops that are on the needle are embraced with an envelope. Repeat this until the ring is completely crocheted. Before you start work, crochet a ring completely to the sample to know how many units are needed overall. This is also dependent on wool strength.

Connect Rings Together

The connection between two rings takes place when the first plastic ring is crocheted in half with solid hands. Now, crochet an air mesh and then the first solid mesh around the next ring.

The last ring of a row is always completely crocheted. All other half-finished crocheted rings will be completed in the second round with solid hands. In doing so, always crochet a solid piece of ash around the connecting air mesh. In the end, pull the thread through the last stitch and sew it.

The second row of rings can also be half crocheted and connected to the rings of the first row. When crocheting the first half of the second row of rings, add the already finished first row of rings. To do this, crochet a slip stitch into the middle stitch of the already finished ring row.

The crochet with plastic rings is particularly suitable for original placemats, small coasters, and the design of fabric bags, which receive such a special design. Of course, all these suggestions are also suitable for individual gifts.

Chapter 11: Mistakes Crochets Make and Solution

As a beginner, you must come across your fair share of frustrations as you get stuck into your crocheting. Mistakes could happen by not following instructions accurately or simply as a result of practice. Remember, there are certain methods you can adjust slightly to suit you, as long as they don't affect the appearance of your stitches and your pattern.

Learning to crochet can be a wonderful experience, so try not to get too despondent if you don't always manage to do everything properly at first. It is a very time-consuming craft and requires a lot of skill, which you will develop over time. Don't be too hard on yourself and just have fun.

Perhaps you may not be familiar with some of these, depending on how much crocheting you have done up to this point. Read through them and keep them in mind if you ever have any of these challenges in the future.

Inserting your hook into the wrong chain when you start

Don't count the first chain on the hook because it is just a loop; your first proper chain is the first chain from the hook, which is the one next to, and the one after that is the second loop on the hook.

When you use US stitches and when your pattern contains UK pattern terms

This can sometimes be really easy to miss and cause several complications. An easy way to check is to look out for single crochet instruction, as this confirms that your pattern is a US pattern that uses US terminology.

Not considering blocking as an important step

First of all, blocking involves handwashing an item and then pinning it into place on a blocking mat. The reason for doing this is to straighten the item and flatten it if needed. It is possible to machine wash your item. Just use the hand setting. There are times when blocking isn't completely necessary, whereas so for you. If you intend to wash it, then be sure to use the blocked gauge measurements.

Making starting loops using linked chains and not a magic loop

You could use methods for starting your crocheting in the round. The first is to work four or five chain stitches and join them in a circle by using a slipstitch. This is the simplest method.

However, a more effective method is to start loops using a magic circle. The center of the circle is much tighter than that of a regular circle linked by a chain stitch. The important thing to remember is consistency; if you use motifs on any items, only use one method to create them as your work will be tidier. So, try them both and see which one you are more comfortable with using and stick to that method.

Not changing the size of your hook as needed

You may have done this and only realized it when your work didn't look quite right. This can happen when your starting chain is rather tight in comparison to the rest of your work. This is, however, a common mistake among beginners. You must have the right tension in your chain as it forms the foundation of your work.

One solution is to use a slightly larger hook than recommended in your pattern, as this will help you to have a more even tension throughout. It is not necessary to change the size of your hook if your tension is correct. Always be aware of specific crochet hook sizes on your patterns.

Your work seems to be shrinking

If you find that your work is shrinking in places and the shape of your item doesn't look right, then you have probably made an error somewhere. The explanation for a mistake such as this is usually a result of making your first stitch in the incorrect position.

Remember these points:

- For single crochet, the first stitch is inserted into the first stitch of the row above.

- For your other basic stitches, it is the turning chain that is to be counted as the first stitch. Hence, this first stitch is inserted into what is the second one of the previous rows.

Not being able to identify your stitches

It is common for beginners to be so involved in trying to follow the instructions in their patterns that they seldom check to see whether their stitches look the way they should. Never fear, this is quite normal and a mistake made by so many of us. There are lots of different moving parts, and it takes a while to catch your rhythm. When you start crocheting, take a moment to count your stitches and learn what they look like.

Avoiding new techniques because they seem too difficult

If something seems too difficult, look at it more carefully before avoiding it completely. If you can do the basic stitches, you'll be able to handle nearly all the crochet techniques without any problem. You may just need to practice a few times. The steps can sometimes seem a bit intimidating, but if you read through them, you'll see that they are made up of basic instructions. So, don't avoid trying something new, it may be easier than you think, and you'll be able to take your crochet to a new level before you know it!

Not learning enough about yarn

When you start buying yarns, learn as much as you can about them. You will, of course, have to use certain yarns depending on the patterns you are using. But also try to find out which ones are of good quality and don't always go for the cheapest.

Don't realize that your turning chain is the same height as the first stitch in the row

You should be able to see that the starting chain of your row brings the height of your work up to that of the first stitch in that row. For example, a single crochet is one chain, and half double crochet is two chains. Have a look at this the next time you are crocheting.

Not being able to read patterns

Nowadays, one can tend to be a tad bit lazy when it comes to reading patterns. This is because online videos are much quicker and easier to follow for some of us. However, this is not ideal, as one should be able to read patterns. By reading through the pattern steps, you'll be able to create a picture in your mind of what the pattern should look like, and it will give you a better understanding of what you are doing.

Not learning corner-to-corner (C2C) crochet

The C2C method is an important and useful one to learn. You will most definitely use it many times, and it is great for making blankets and other garments. Don't avoid this one; try it and practice. You won't regret what you did.

Not learning how to crochet in the round

It is important to see how this works and then try it. This is vital to improving your crochet skills, so don't put off learning how to crochet in the round. It is a valuable technique to know how to use.

Not learning how to weave in ends properly

This is one of the most common mistakes made by beginners. It is so easy to just tie knots to the ends, but this is not the proper way of doing it, and it is not neat either. Learn to weave the ends into the surface by using the tapestry needle to finish your work off.

Worrying about your mistakes

Making mistakes is what helps you to learn and improve your work. Lots of practice and even more patience, as well as some creativity, is what makes a successful crocheter. You will have to undo your stitches from time to time or even start over again, but that is fine. You are not only learning how to follow instructions;

you are also getting used to using your tools and materials, so be patient.

Trying out complex patterns first

So often, ladies are in a hurry to create the most beautiful colorful garments without being able to master the stitches or change their yarn colors. This could result in a disaster that could also be incredibly discouraging. Just keep it simple until you are confident with basic crochet work.

Giving up too soon

It is too easy to just pick up your crochet hook, try out a few stitches, and then give up if they don't work. You might feel as though you are getting nowhere, but that is not true. Give yourself plenty of time to learn the basics because once you can do that, then you can move forward and make so many items. If you cannot get your basic stitches right, then you will have problems making your item. Take it easy, and things will slowly start coming together.

Even the most skillful people struggled at first, so go for it and enjoy it!

Some Crocheting Mistakes and How to Avoid Them

Ruling out completely the possibility of errors in a beginner's work is impossible. Even people who have been doing crochet for long are still susceptible to some of these mistakes. These errors can, however, be mitigated. Some of these mistakes are:

Using a different yarn weight from the one instructed

Yarns are not all the same; they vary in color, materials, and weights. You should check the instructions to know the correct one to use so that you won't be 'wowed' by your crochet piece when it is done.

Not counting your stitches and rows as you go along your crochet work

To lessen the pain (lol) that is often associated with frogging, try to count your rows and stitches as you work. A digital row counter can be of great help.

Not understanding the how-to of a project before embarking on it

In relative terms, crochet work takes time. So, why not know what to do before you start? I will advise beginners to always read through pattern instructions before putting the hook to the yarn.

This will help you to avoid unnecessary stress as you continue in the project. It will also help to reduce the incidence of frogging or even having to abandon the entire project.

Working with one loop only

It is not uncommon for beginners to only slide the hooks under one of the loops and neglect the other one. Except the instruction says otherwise, it is better to work with both loops.

Misplacing the first stitch

You should learn where to place the first stitches in each row. There are instances where the instruction says to use the second or third stitch and not the first. Putting it at the wrong place might only make you have an irregular shape; it might even give a result that is totally different from the one anticipated, and you have to reclaim the entire yarn.

Not paying attention to US and UK terms

Instructions might be written in either of the two, and the responsibility falls on the crocheter to know which is which. If you use a UK stitch where the instruction was written in US terms, and you don't make the necessary amendments, you might end up mixing up a double crochet stitch with a single and vice versa.

Not weaving in (Fastening off) properly

This will unravel all you have done if you are not careful.

Using a Crochet Gauge

It is not uncommon for a beginner crocheter to find out that his or her crochet piece is different from the one predicted by the instructions followed. It might be bigger or smaller. A crochet gauge is a very good tool for a beginner to get the expected result.

What does a crochet gauge do? Just like the name implies, a crochet gauge 'gauges' crochet projects. It specifies measurements in crochet by indicating the number of stitches per centimeter or inch.

How to use a crochet gauge

1. Before you start a crochet project, look for the gauge aspect of the instructions. Read and understand it.

2. Make your base chain to be a little bit longer than the length recommended by the gauge.

3. Get the correct hook size and yarn weight* by following the instructions. Yarn might be light or bulky or in between the two. Try to get the one specified by the instruction.

Note: The weight of your yarn = the thickness of your yarn. It is not the weight of the ball or skein of yarn that you have. You can check the yarn pack. It should be written there.

Chapter 12: Crocheting Background

Knitted fabrics are said to have been in existence since earlier times. However, its origin is unclear since the skill has mostly been spread verbally between interested parties. They would copy the crochet pattern from someone's original work. This would result in different types of crochet mistakes, hence no perfection of any of the styles.

Research states that crocheting may have started in china through their needlework, which was a very common practice in Turkey and India as well as in North America. It is after this that the crocheting methods reached Europe, but they would refer to it as a tambourine. Tambourine later evolved to 'crocheting in the air' since the fabric used in the background had to be removed for the stitch to stand on its own.

Crocheted fabrics became popular in Europe in the 19th century. Instructions about crocheting were first published in a magazine in the year 1823. The magazine had detailed information about the color plate that contained different styles. After publishing the magazine, the first crochet patterns were printed in 1824.

Mlle. Riego de la Branchardiere is said to have contributed a lot to the popularity of crocheting in Europe. This is as a result of the patterns books that she published in the 1800s, which were so easy to duplicate. The pattern books were given to millions of women who had an interest in crocheting. This was a sure way to ensure that the patterns reached as many women as possible, whether they could afford the books or not.

Many women around the world started copying the patterns, which made crocheting so popular. There are a lot of materials that one can learn from on the internet. One can, therefore, learn about crocheting from websites and different sites on the internet. Different crochet pattern books have also been published that contain different and unique crochet styles. Therefore, it is evident that crocheting has greatly evolved, which has made it so popular. Many modern crocheted clothing is already being sold in our markets worldwide.

What Makes Someone Think of Crocheting?

Many people around the world have mastered the art of crocheting. This is as a result of the many benefits that come with it. Some people will, however, crochet for different reasons. There are many people out there who may be wondering why people crochet. They do not see enough reason why you should spend their free time crocheting. Most times, they lack the motivation to start crocheting, so it would be great if I highlight a few reasons for crocheting.

Crocheting Is a Stress Reliever

Crocheting has been tried and proven to be one of the activities that help people to relieve stress. This is because as you crochet, you can forget all the problems you may be going through. All your concentration is on the pattern making, so all your mind is occupied. As you crochet, all that is in your mind evaporates, which helps a lot in relaxing your mind. Whenever one needs to learn a new crocheting skill, they have to go through different books, sites, and also apps that normally engage them mindfully. One forgets everything they are going through since they are curious to learn a new skill.

Crocheting Brings a Great Sense of Accomplishment

There is no better feeling than seeing people wear or cover themselves with items that you crocheted yourself. It makes you feel great about the time you spent crocheting the items. It isn't a waste of time as you can see them enjoy the fruits of your labor. That feeling is so fulfilling that you will want to keep crocheting. You will also keep on discovering new patterns, and after implementing the skill, you will have a great sense of fulfillment.

Crocheting Enables You to Have an Alert Mind

People grow older each day. Crocheting offers a lasting solution to people who would want to remain alert as well as stimulated. One has to remain alert, especially when they are working on a new pattern. Therefore, isn't it important to engage our minds with crocheting?

Keeping the Tradition Alive

We mostly inherit the crocheting skills from our parents, aunts, and even from our grandmothers. It would be a great thing to keep the tradition alive by passing it on to the people around us. It is very important to ensure that we pass down the crocheting art to our children and even the people around us. For every crochet, there is some bit of love from the people we learn this art form.

Crocheting Keeps You Busy

Whenever one is crocheting, their mind is fully engaged. This means that they are busy, hence will not be thinking about anything else. Being busy is beneficial in that one won't be idling around without doing any meaningful thing. For most people, crocheting is a hobby, so they use their free time doing it.

Enhancing Your Creativity

We learn a new trick every day. Through crocheting, one can perfect their skills by designing new patterns. They can creatively mix different color schemes to come up with beautiful patterns, which make the crochets to be more appealing. It is through crocheting that one can experience a comforting effect from the great textures created through the repeated movements using yarns of different colors.

Health Benefit

Apart from relieving stress, crocheting is of great benefit to people suffering from arthritis. This is because as one works through various stitches, the fingers remain nimble, hence reduce the risks of arthritis. People who get Alzheimer's attacks are also advised to consider engaging in crocheting. This is because they can reduce the attacks by a great percentage. Whenever they engage themselves in learning a new skill, they get to preserve some of the memories they have made in the past.

The Economic Part of Crocheting

Many people around the world have been able to learn crocheting skills. It is an industry that has grown and has empowered many men and women around the world. This has greatly improved the economy. Do crotchets have an economic impact? Several people may not find crocheting beneficial. They may not see it as a source of income, but it contributes immensely to the economy.

During cold seasons people look for warm things to keep them warm. They, therefore, have to purchase scarves, sweaters, socks, and other products made from yarn. This increases the rate of yarn production as a result of the increase in demand for crocheted items. This is said to lead to the growth of the economy. Below are some of the economic impacts brought by crocheting.

So many crocheting companies have been opened, which has created employment opportunities for many families around the world. They can take care of their families from the income they earn from the crocheting companies.

Women can crochet items and sell them to people in their neighborhood, which enables them to earn some income. This helps to improve the economy since they do not become dependent on the government for their survival. Therefore, the government can concentrate on other development projects since its people are not overly dependent on them.

People have also been able to come up with unique patterns and have published them in books that are later sold to interested parties. This acts as a source of income for the publisher, which also helps in the growth of the economy.

The experts in this area have also taken up the role of training more people in crocheting. This ensures the empowerment of more people, which means more skilled individuals in a country.

Individuals who have specialized in information technology also develop apps that contain crochet instructions. This has helped people to have easy access to the skills, so anyone can install the app and learn the skills in their own free time.

Social and Traditional Impact of Crocheting

Crocheting has had a great impact on our society. The skill keeps on being passed on from one generation to another. This has helped a lot in impacting people's lives socially and even traditionally. Below are some social and traditional impacts brought by crocheting.

For Charity

Often, we find ourselves with different types of crotchets that we mostly make during our free time. One can craft some items and give them out to charities. It will always feel great when one benefits from an item crocheted with a lot of love. It will act as a way of showing your generosity and sense of care for others. One will feel good when someone appreciates something that was made purposely to suit their need.

Aesthetic Value

Crocheting can display the beauty of a tradition. Before the invention of big companies that dealt with the manufacturing of clothes, people used to wear crocheted clothes. Some people make crochets to beautify the environment. Therefore, someone makes items that they are sure will make their environment calm. This will enable them to feel relaxed whenever they are around.

Boost Self-Esteem

We all feel good when complimented for doing something so well. Compliments motivate us to produce better crochets that are better than the previous ones. When we sell the crafts, we made or give it as a gift, and it boosts your self-esteem. You feel great about your accomplishments. Self-esteem can also be built through learning new skills. One can feel productive, which creates beauty through self-expression.

Reduces Stress and Anxiety

We all get stressed up at some point in our life. We may feel anxious as a result of the strenuous activities we may have engaged in on our daily activities. One needs to give themselves a break. Getting a yarn and crochet would be of great help in relaxing their mind. It is through the repetition of the stitches as you count the rows that your mind gets some kind of relaxation. All the anxiety thoughts are set free since your focus is on creatively making the crochets.

Eases and Relieves Depression

Our emotions keep changing, depending on the occasion. For instance, in the grieving period, it seems impossible to overcome your grief. Most times, we feel like the world has come to an end. Crocheting can be a comforter during the grieving period. Crafting such as crocheting is said to be helpful in the stimulation of dopamine, which enables one to feel happier and emotionally stable.

Keeps You Busy

Imagine you are left at home alone. No other work for you, you can choose to do some crocheting. You will be relaxing at the same time, keeping yourself busy. You don't have to create wonderful products out of it. The whole idea is to keep your mind engaged through a useful course, which may help you earn some income or even contribute to charity. In a scenario where you are following a program on television, your hands will be busy crafting while your eyes are glued to the television. The best thing about crocheting is that one can engage every member of the family. They will be able to contribute with various ideas about what you are making and suggestions on colors and even designs.

Brings Communities Together

There are many ways to bring people together. One of them is having yarn crafting introduced to a community. They can have a meeting in public to do crocheting. Organizers can plan a fiber fair together with related events. This will be of great help since people from different places will be able to meet and share ideas. They will be able to learn from one another, hence more creative designs. The community can even come together and build yarn stores, which will benefit the community from the sales made in the store. All the participants can also buy the yarn at a reduced price that will enable them to make more crocheted items for sale. They, in return, become more productive, which brings economic empowerment amongst them.

Conclusion

Crochet is one of the most beautiful and fun arts you can learn.

Initially, it will be tiring, especially when various attempts fail. It is precisely then that you will not have to give up and try and try again until you reach the desired result.

Get inspired and carry out projects starting from the simplest to ending with advanced projects that you will be happy to show everyone. Thanks to the basics learned here; this is within your reach.

If you like, leave me feedback on Amazon.com and show me your masterpieces, I will be happy with it.

Good Luck!

CPSIA information can be obtained
at www.ICGtesting.com
Printed in the USA
LVHW081542140221
679289LV00052B/768